W9-BWP-126

ZERO-BASE BUDGETING FOR PUBLIC PROGRAMS, REVISED EDITION

ST. JOSEPH'S UNIVERSITY   STX
HJ2052.D7 1980
Zero-base budgeting for public programs

3 9353 00102 8685

Frank D. Draper
Bernard T. Pitsvada

HJ
2052
.D7
1980

192209

 University Press of America™

Copyright © 1980 by

University Press of America, Inc.™

4710 Auth Place, S.E., Washington, D.C. 20023

All rights reserved

Printed in the United States of America

ISBN: 0-8191-0719-0

Library of Congress Number: 79-63503

PREFACE

Since it was first popularized by then-Presidential candidate Jimmy Carter, Zero-Base Budgeting (ZBB) has been the subject of much discussion. While there are previous works which deal with ZBB -- primarily in the private sector -- nothing has been written that places this newest budget innovation in perspective within public sector budgeting exclusively. This book attempts to address that need. In addition to illustrating the mechanics of how ZBB is performed in government, the book also places ZBB in its historical and theoretical context, assesses its benefits and costs, and explores the problems and prospects of ZBB as they exist today. In this undertaking the book draws on the experiences to date of ZBB's use in the public sector.

As such then the book can serve several purposes. It is designed to be used as a handbook for personnel involved in actually doing ZBB -- it was written by persons who actually prepare government budgets -- as well as a text in the classroom for instruction in the field of public administration. Further, it can be used as a supplement to training given in ZBB.

One caveat is in order. ZBB is a flexible system; it must be adapted to the needs of agencies. The illustration used here as to how ZBB might be performed in a government agency is taken from the National Science Foundation. However, the illustration is just one way the process can be implemented. The "decision units," "decision packages," and the "rankings" displayed do not necessarily represent the process in the NSF, nor do the comments and criticisms reflect the official position of the NSF (or the Department of Army).

iii

Needless to say, the views are the authors' own -- we readily claim them.

As a final word, thanks is due to the Office of Planning and Resources Management of the NSF for alerting the authors to what possibly may be the next stage in budget reform, "historical incrementalism." Further, special thanks is due Mary for typing the manuscript so as to assure its timely reception.

TABLE OF CONTENTS

INTRODUCTION

With the election of President Carter there has been much talk recently -- perhaps "clamor" might be a better word -- concerning the next stage in budget innovation, Zero-Base Budgeting. It would seem that together with "Performance Budgeting," "PPB" (Planning-Programing-Budgeting), and "MBO" (Management by Objectives), we must now add "ZBB."

Like previous budget innovations, the underlying aim of ZBB is to insert rationality into the budgetary process: the establishment of a formalized system in the budget cycle that will <u>assist</u> us in judiciously allocating our nation's resources. A system which will <u>help</u> us in somehow maximizing what economists like to call our "social welfare function" and also attempting "pareto-optimum solutions" -- or, in simple terms, a mechanism which will <u>aid</u> the decision makers in divining the proper mix of guns and butter that will most benefit societal needs and fulfill desires. (The emphasis is on "assistance," "help," and "aid," since no system -- though perhaps some of the most strident critics of the PPB System might disagree -- has ever claimed to be a "black box" from which optimal resource allocation decisions can be methodically obtained.)

Further, ZBB, which in theory at least means justifying each program from the ground up, is marshalling wide support. Not only did President Carter, on February 14, 1977, direct all Executive departments and agencies to implement ZBB, beginning with the Fiscal Year 1979 budget, but Congress as well is leaning toward its own form of ZBB, so-called "Sunset" legislation. Under such legislation (the most recent and notable being the Muskie bill, S.2., introduced very early in the 95th Congress), the "sun would set" automatically every six years on Federal programs which did not prove themselves deserving of continued funding. Designed to address, among other things, the increasing percentage taken each year by the "uncontrollable" portion of the Federal budget -- "uncontrollable" outlays have risen from 59% in FY 1967 to over 77% in FY 1977 -- enactment of the legislation would provide additional impetus to the recent reassertion by Congress in setting national priorities. The mystique of ZBB has also engulfed state budgeting systems: one recent analysis by the Congressional Research Service of the Library of Congress noted that eleven states had already implemented ZBB, and estimated that nearly one-half of all the states would have aspects of a zero-base budgeting system in place by 1980. Finally, while no assessment has as yet been made of ZBB inroads into local government budgetary processes, still its use there is also thought to be substantial.

With the groundswell of interest in ZBB in the Federal establishment as well as in state and local governments, it might be safe to say that ZBB will be with us for a while. It would seem appropriate, then, that we examine in detail the concept of ZBB. More specifically,

- What is ZBB?

- How does it work?

- What are its benefits and costs? And how does it fit with other budget innovations?

- What are the problems and prospects for ZBB?

However, before beginning, we must first explore public budgeting from historical and theoretical perspectives. For ZBB is a very eclectic system; it trades very heavily on aspects of budget innovations of the past. Only when this eclecticism is perceived can the significance of ZBB be gauged, and some sense of its future evolution be obtained.

CHAPTER ONE

Budgeting -- A Historical Perspective

It has been observed numerous times in recent years that the twentieth century has not been kind to the functioning of legislative bodies around the world. This century, it is maintained, has been a century of executive power, executive action and the expansion of executive authority. In a general sense this appears to be true. The significant growth of executive power that we have witnessed in American politics since the early 1930's has to a great extent been matched by a comparable decline in Congressional influence, direction and purpose. The relative shift in power between Congress and the Executive is noticeable in many areas of government policy but probably the most significant one is that which relates to the Congressional "power of the purse." As one source says. "The power of the purse is the historic bulwark of legislative authority. The exercise of that power constitutes the core legislative process -- underpinning all other legislative decisions and regulating the balance of influence between the legislative and executive branches of government."[1] Nevertheless, despite its recognized importance to the total structure of legislative government, Congress has in the last forty odd years lost much of its control over this vital power. In fact the decline of legislative power in America can in many ways be traced to Congress' loss of control over its constitutionally granted fiscal functions, from the raising of revenue to the appropriating of funds. Congress has recognized that the heart of its exercise of the power of the purse revolves around its budgetary functions and the decisions it makes during the so-called budgetary process. To this end in 1974, Congress passed legislation to remedy what it interpreted as its major shortcomings in the process of allocating national resources to competing claims. It will be interesting over the next decade to view the development of the new budgetary process to determine if it will reverse the tide of ebbing Congressional power, if indeed such a reversal is possible.

Comparatively speaking budgeting is one of the more complex functions that governments perform. In western political development budgeting can be traced historically to the first attempts of a type of representative body to approve or disapprove of the executive's plans to raise taxes. Hence budgeting has had a representative or legislative basis from the outset. In addition, as corollaries to the development of representative government, budgeting can be viewed as an outgrowth of attempts of citizens to curb unbridled executive power and to develop a concept of government of limited powers.

In English political history the single event most directly related to these developments was the granting of the Magna Carta in 1215. King John, under provisions of this historic agreement, obligated himself to obtain the approval of his barons before imposing certain taxes on his subjects. However, as is the case with most innovative governmental practices, the development and evolution of budgeting through various stages of seven centuries of British history was not a continuous string of successes or achievements. The evolutionary process of approving the raising of revenue, approving expenditures of the Crown and finally developing an annual financial plan based on revenues and expenditures was a long time in coming. Buck maintains that English budgetary development went through these three distinct phases and only reached the final phase at the beginning of the eighteenth century.[2] Nevertheless the outcome was as Burkhead states, "...the long struggle for Parliamentary control of the purse was a struggle for control over taxation. The control over expenditure came much later, and as a by-product of the concern for the protection of taxpayers."[3]

The influence of English political thought and

practice on American political development has, of
course, been profound and far reaching. The fields of
legislative control of taxation, distrust of executive
power and by extension, budgeting, were no exceptions.
Added to these attitudes was an unswerving faith in the
local control of political affairs. Since many Colonial
governors were appointed by the Crown while legislatures consisted of local leaders, it is not surprising
that the colonists placed far more trust in locally
elected legislatures than they did in their appointed
executives, especially in matters of taxation.

It was this very issue of taxation that finally
triggered the chain of events that led to American independence. A harmless appearing Stamp Act to which
King George gave his approval in March 1765 was greeted
by what Rossiter refers to as "overwhelming refusal to
obey, especially among colonial leaders who saw ruin
in its provisions."4 After protests from the colonies
the noxious stamp tax was replaced in 1767 by a tax on
glass, dye and tea which in turn was replaced by a tea
tax on 1770. Nevertheless the concessions on the part
of Parliament and the Crown were to no avail. Stourm
has said that these events became "the signal for the
War of Independence, because the American people held
out for a vital principle."5 Whether the Colonists were
concerned more with principle or pocketbook is not as
important as the fact that they declared independence
and organized to fight to secure it.

The Colonists established a basically executive-
less government under the Articles of Confederation
in 1777. This type of government was a reflection of
Colonial attitudes toward the legislative branch and
the disfavor in which executives were held. Nevertheless, the approach proved impractical in most areas
including that of raising revenue and authorizing expenditures. A system of Committees composed of members
of Congress was tried as was the establishment of
boards composed of individuals outside of Congress as
means of improving administration. Finally when the
Constitution was drafted, it called for a separate
executive, an independent judiciary and two houses of
Congress.

In examining the proceedings of the Constitutional
Convention and the arguments for the approval of the
new Constitution stated in The Federalist, there is
virtually no discussion whatsoever about a budget, a
budgetary system or budgetary practices. As might be

expected there was a vigorous concern about taxes. Nevertheless even in this case the Constitution as it was finally written merely included a general procedural provision regarding withdrawal of funds from the Treasury. This was to occur only as a result of a legal appropriation by Congress. In addition periodic publication of statements of receipts and expenditures were required. Similarly in Federalist #36, in which Alexander Hamilton expressed his feelings concerning internal taxation, his observations about what can be considered the practice of budgeting are basically procedural as they relate to raising taxes. He observed that most nations generally assigned the administration of finances to a single man or boards "...who digest and prepare, in the first instance, the plans of taxation, which are afterwards passed into laws by the authority of the sovereign or legislature."[6]

A lack of discussion on the part of our Founding Fathers, however, was no impediment to developing the actual practice of budgeting. To implement the Constitutional provisions regarding financial affairs and reporting, Congress passed an act on September 2, 1789 establishing the Treasury Department. Earlier legislation had created a Department of Foreign Affairs and a Department of War. These three agencies comprised the first cabinet. The Act of September 2 made the Secretary of the Treasury responsible to prepare and report to Congress regarding estimates of revenue and expenditures. The exact form of these reports was not specified nor was there any requirement that the revenues and expenditures be included in the same report.[7]

Alexander Hamilton was selected by George Washington to be the first Secretary of Treasury. In fact in terms of the date of selection Hamilton was actually the first Cabinet Secretary appointed by Washington.[8] As Secretary of Treasury, Hamilton prepared and submitted to the Congress a budget for the year 1790.[9] For the years of his tenure Hamilton presented a unified budget to Congress either in person or, as it later evolved, over his signature. The budget included all the expenses of the government except for those of the Army which appeared in the budget under the signature of Secretary of War Knox. During this period the dealings between Hamilton and the Congress were directly with the separate bodies of the legislature as a whole, i.e., with the House and the Senate. Hamilton's working relationship with Congress, however, was anything but smooth and tranquil most likely because of his expansive views of executive power and executive discretion . On one occasion, he was actually charged by a House resolution in 1793 with violating appropriation laws, ignoring Presidential instructions and even failing to discharge his duties.[10] Hamilton's vigorous execution of his office continued to evoke a great deal of criticism from Congress and finally in December 1974 he resigned. Two years later in what was probably a Congressional reaction to the Hamiltonian conception of executive power and certainly was an attempt to involve Congress more directly in the budgetary process, the House made an organizational change which according to Buck, "...practically ended executive initiative in budgetary matters."[11] The House created a standing Committee on Ways and Means which placed itself between the Executive and the House as a whole. The Committee did not become a permanent standing committee until 1802, nevertheless its functioning since 1796 virtually ended the direct contact between Congress and the Executive. The Committee on Ways and Means which was granted authority over both revenues and appropriations became the central Congressional figure in the budgetary process.

In addition Congress passed an act in May 1800 which directed the Secretary of Treasury "to digest, prepare and lay before Congress" a report dealing with revenues and expenditures as well as plans for increasing revenues. This piece of legislation in a sense reflected Congress' ambivalent attitude toward the Treasury Department. By requiring the Secretary of the Treasury to report periodically to Congress there was a clear implication of a unique quasi-legislative nature to the functions of the Treasury Department. The other existing cabinet officers had no such similar responsibility to report directly to Congress. The law also provided what in the hands of a vigorous Secretary could have been the framework for a unified executive budget, much like the one Hamilton tried to establish. However, the unwillingness of Congress in practice to grant the executive branch broad appropriations, the desire of Congress to organize a standing Committee structure, and the somewhat anti-executive political philosophy of the Jeffersonians tipped the pendulum in the direction of legislative control of the budget. This was further accelerated by the developing practice of precluding the Secretary of Treasury from amending agency estimates for funds. The Secretary became a transmitter to Congress of individual agency requests and not a reviewing authority responsible for developing a unified budget. This practice was later

converted into formal legislation.[12] The only exception to this emerging legislative dominance during the
1800-1812 period was the case of Albert Gallatin, who
served as Jefferson's Secretary of Treasury. Gallatin
had some influence in working with the House Ways and
Means Committee, but the probable reason for this was
that he had been a member of the Ways and Means Committee before moving into the executive branch. As a result his influence was personal, not institutional, and
therefore lapsed with his departure.

The congressional dominance of the appropriation
and budgetary process continued almost without challenge for the next half century. Of all the Chief
Executives only Andrew Jackson, with his struggles over
the Second Bank of the United States, and James K. Polk,
a former Chairman of the House Ways and Means Committee, attempted to exert meaningful influence over
the budget and expenditures. Polk actively participa-
ted in reviewing budget estimates with his cabinet
members and attempted to reduce the estimates to as
low a level as was possible.[13] Despite these attempts
the initiative in the budget area rested with Congress.
However, the Civil War with its vast increase in expenditures strained the existing Committee structure
in both houses of Congress. As a result, in 1865 the
House altered the jurisdiction of the Ways and Means
Committee and in 1867 the Senate did the same with its
Finance Committee. Both houses established separate
appropriation committees which assumed the responsibility of allocating expenditures. Only revenue raising remained with the House Ways and Means and Senate
Finance Committees. This change in congressional committee structure ended the last semblance of unity
anywhere in the budget process. The trend toward
fragmentation was further compounded in 1885 when six
areas of appropriations were removed from the House
Appropriations Committee jurisdiction. The areas were
consular and diplomatic affairs, Army, Navy, Military
Academy, Post Office and Indian Affairs. Earlier,
rivers and harbors and agriculture and forestry had
similarly been removed from Appropriations Committee
jurisdiction.[14] By the beginning of the twentieth
century the various executive bureaus were independently submitting their budget requests to specialized
committees in Congress, with neither central executive
direction regarding the total size of the budget nor
unified congressional control exerted over the total
level of appropriations or the relationship of revenues
to expenditures. The result was disunity and virtually

uncontrolled expenditure of public revenues.

Despite what appears to have been a chaotic, free-for-all system for reaching budgetary allocations, there was little public or governmental agitation for change until the turn of the century. A general degree of satisfaction on the part of all of the participants in the budgetary process and the body politic can be inferred from the absence of criticism during the half century following the Civil War. The most likely reason for this general state of satisfaction was that during this period of American history there was usually adequate funding available for virtually all existing programs and claims for additional programs.

Budgeting begins to take on significance only when demands exceed resources, i.e., when there is competition for scarce resources. From 1866 to 1893 the government recorded budgetary surpluses each year and concern was occasionally voiced by politicians and businessmen about how to dispose of the surplus. It was not until a series of six budget deficits in the years 1894 to 1899 that concern about the allocation of resources began to become widespread.

The situation at the beginning of the twentieth century has been described by one source as follows:
> By 1900, however, existing revenue sources no longer consistently produced sufficient sums to cover the costs of government. At the federal level, the tariff could not be expected to produce a surplus of funds as had been the case. Causes of this growing deficit were an expanded scope of governmental programs and, to a lesser extent waste and corruption in government finance.15

Budgetary surpluses from 1900 to 1903 were followed by deficits in 1904 and 1905. Surpluses were recorded the next two years but again deficits followed the next three. In response to this fluctuating budgetary picture, Congress enacted a provision in the Sundry Civil Expenses Appropriation Act in 1909 which required the Secretary of the Treasury to inform Congress if in any year appropriations exceeded revenues, how appropriations could be reduced "with least injury to the public service" and, if such a reduction could not be made, the Secretary was to recommend to

the Congress what loans or taxes would be required to
cover the deficiency. This was another instance where
legislation was passed that could have gone a long way
to reassert executive control over the total level of
resources requested in a budget. However, as Burkhead
noted "...there is no evidence that the Secretary of
the Treasury ever acted in conformity with this direc-
tive."16 Naylor attributes the "non-use" of this provision to the fact that the presidents had never used
the Treasury Department for such a purpose and there
was no other agency through which the president could
have exercised such authority.17

      While President Taft made no use of the authority
granted to him in the Sundry Civil Expenses Appropriation Act, he did request an appropriation of $100,000
in order that a study be made on how to improve the
transaction of public business as it was then conducted by the executive branch. Congress granted the
appropriation in 1910 and Taft accordingly appointed
five members to a body that was called the Commission
on Economy and Efficiency. The Chairman of the Commission was Frederick A. Cleveland, a man well known
for his budgetary reform work at the municipal level.
The Commission remained in operation for two years
studying a whole spectrum of governmental budgetary
practices and management procedures. The Commission
eventually produced a report calling for an executive
budget, a proposal that would have drastically changed
the Federal government's existing budgetary operation.
Taft presented the Commission's recommendation to
Congress in June 1912. The Commission proposal, which
he vigorously supported,would have replaced the practice of each agency submitting its budget request
directly to Congress by requiring that agency budget
requests be submitted to the President, who after review would compile the separate requests into a comprehensive request for a total executive budget that
represented the President's plan for action. The proposal for an executive budget along with the development of the first organizational chart of the executive branch that the Commission prepared were highly
significant matters in US budgetary history. However,
as Burkhead says of the Commission report and Taft's
message to Congress, "Of eve greater significance was
the fact that these documents represented an assumption
of responsibility by the Chief Executive for financial
planning and for the management of the 'government's
business' as it was then called."18 Taft's proposals
called for nothing less than returning the executive

to the center of the federal budgetary stage.

Taft moved ahead to implement the Commission's recommendation in June 1912 by directing the various executive agencies to prepare one set of budget estimates in the traditional manner for submission to Congress and the second set according to the manner recommended by the Commission for submission to the President who would then submit them to Congress. However, Taft and the Republican Party had lost control of the House in the 1910 elections to the Democrats. As a result, his recommendations for drastic revision of the budgetary process had little chance of being accepted. Taft's own report on the work of the Commission was referred to Democratic-controlled congressional committees who took no action on the proposals. Congress, in apparent retaliation for Taft's initiatives, approved an act in August 1912 which required executive branch employees to prepare budget estimates in the manner prescribed by law only. While this was designed to stop the preparation of the "reform" budget, the Taft administration proceeded to move ahead with its plans. As a result, the budget for the fiscal year July 1, 1913 to June 30, 1914 was submitted to Congress in both formats, the traditional manner as required by law and the reform manner as recommended by the Commission and President Taft. Congress dutifully ignored the new reform budget submission and considered the budget estimates in the traditional manner.

The election of Woodrow Wilson in 1912 temporarily stalled the forces of budget reform. While Wilson had a philosophic commitment to budget reform, he had no vested interest as did Taft in the existing proposals then being discussed. The passage of the 16th Amendment and the resulting flow of additional money made available by the income tax also temporarily eased the need for better financial management. Added to these elements were Wilson's emphasis on international affairs and the coming of World War I. These factors combined to make budget reform at the national level temporarily a matter of secondary importance. Nevertheless by 1916 both major parties as well as the Progressive Party made support for various types of budgetary reform one of the elements of their party platforms.

Of the three parties contesting the 1916 election the winning Democrats had the least drastic of the budgetary reform proposals. It merely called for return to the single Appropriations Committee concept that prevailed before the 1880's. As a result when President Wilson turned to domestic considerations at the conclusion of World War I, it was this proposal that he advocated rather than the Taft proposal. However, time had overtaken such a modest reform proposal and in July 1919 the House created a twelve man Select Committee on the Budget which favorably reported a bill establishing an executive budget. The bill was passed by the House in October 1919 but the Senate never considered the measure until the following year. In the interim, President Wilson announced his support for the House proposal.

The report of the House Select Committee probably provides the most comprehensive analysis of the defects of the existing system and what the new bill was designed to accomplish. The report listed among the defects of the present system:

> ...Expenditures are not considered
> in connection with revenues; that
> Congress does not require of the
> President any carefully thought-out
> financial and work program represent-
> ing what provision in his opinion
> should be made for meeting the finan-
> cial needs of the government; that the
> estimates of expenditure needs now
> submitted to Congress represent only
> the desires of the individual depart-
> ments, establishments, and bureaus;
> and that these requests have been
> subjected to no superior revision with
> a view to bringing them into harmony
> with each other, to eliminating dupli-
> cation of organization or activities,
> or of making them, as a whole, conform
> to the needs of the Nation as represented
> by the condition of the Treasury and
> prospective revenues.[19]

The report continued that the current budget estimates were a "patchwork and not a structure" and that the committees of Congress which reviewed these estimates had to spend a great deal of time "...exploding the visionary schemes of bureau chiefs for which no administration would be willing to stand responsible."[20] The Select Committee concluded that if economy and efficiency in the expenditure of funds was ever to be accomplished "the only way by which

this can be done is by placing definite responsibility
upon some officer of the Government to receive the
requests for funds as originally formulated by bureau
and department chiefs and subjecting them to scrutiny,
revision, and correlation that has been described. In
the National Government there can be no question but
that the officer upon whom should be placed this responsibility is the President of the United States."[21]
The report also indicated that the new budgetary
system would not give the President any greater power
than he had over appropriations and similarly did not
reduce the duty of Congress to review budget submissions in detail.[22]

In addition to requiring the submission of an
executive budget, the bill as it passed the House
established a bureau of the budget to assist the
President in budget preparation and an independent
accounting department to furnish information to
Congress regarding expenditures of the government. The
accounting department, which later evolved into the
General Accounting Office, was placed under the direction of the Comptroller General who was to be appointed
with the advice and consent of the Senate and hold
office during good behavior. He was to be removable
only by concurrent resolution of Congress on such
grounds as inefficiency, neglect of duty or malfea-
sance in office.

The Committee concluded with a tribute to ortho-
doxy by noting that the bill was an evolutionary step
rather than any revolutionary change in governmental
operations and it was no departure from the fundamental political principles of the present government.

The Senate similarly considered the proposals for
budget reform by appointing a Special Committee on the
National Budget chaired by Senator Medill McCormick.
McCormick's Committee favorably reported the House
version, with changes, in April 1920. The Committee
report observed that the requirement for reform was so
obvious that there was no need to present the arguments in its favor in the report. The report noted
that the only problem was one of "...method - of how
best to adopt the budget idea to our existing practices in financial administration."[23] The Senate bill
proposed to establish the bureau of the budget as part
of the Treasury Department, not as part of the Office
of the President as the House bill proposed. In
addition, the Senate version increased the powers of

the Comptroller General. The differences in the versions of the bills were resolved, and Congress gave final approval to the bill in May 1920.

However, on June 4, 1920 President Wilson vetoed the bill because of his objection to the placement of the Comptroller General beyond the removal power of the President. Wilson indicated in his veto message that, while he supported the objectives of the bill, he considered the provision dealing with the Comptroller General as unconstitutional because it gave Congress, and not the President, authority to remove the Comptroller General from office. Wilson's message indicated that he viewed the power of removal as incident to the power to appoint and in his view this was clearly an executive power.

The election of Warren Harding in 1920 and the change of the party in power did not slow the process of budgetary reform as it had in the past. Congress reconsidered the bill after it convened in 1921 and repassed it with minimal change as the Budget and Accounting Act of 1921. Harding signed the bill into law in June 1921. In addition to the reform in the executive branch that resulted from the Budget and Accounting Act, Congress made some internal rules changes which were designed to consolidate Congressional review of the budget. In June 1920 the House returned to establishing one Committee for revenue (Ways and Means) and only one Committee for appropriations. The Senate followed suit in 1922. However, the fact that appropriation committees were consolidated was somewhat negated by the fact that the committees soon established sub-committees which acted on various segments of the budget with considerable independence. In addition, the Senate permitted the chairman and other ranking members of substantive policy committees to participate in appropriations committee proceedings. As a result, congressional centralization of budget review was somewhat short-lived and in the end more form than substance.

On the other hand, the executive branch moved toward both the form and substance of centralization. Soon after his appointment the first Director of the Budget, Charles G. Dawes sought from President Harding the authority to summon various cabinet members to meet with him regarding budgetary matters. Dawes, as head of the Bureau of the Budget, was a subordinate of the Secretary of Treasury yet he requested authority

-14-

to summon higher ranking government officials including the Secretary of Treasury to meet with him. President Harding resolved the matter by agreeing with
Dawes, but he directed that the conferences between
Dawes and cabinet officials be held in the White House
rather than in Dawes' office. This lent an air of
presidential authority to the meetings and at the same
time demonstrated an extent of executive control of the
budget.

Another major indication of the rapidly expanding
executive centralization over the budget appeared in
Dawes' evaluation of the preparation of the budget for
the fiscal year July 1, 1922 to June 30, 1923. Dawes
indicated that the Bureau of the Budget's most prominent activity in that first year of operations had been
reducing the requests for expenditures of various
agencies. In this way the Bureau acted to curb what
it interpreted as the extravagances of the executive
departments.[24] Such action represented a major departure from the previous methods of submitting un-
coordinated and independent agency budget requests to
Congress. However, the emphasis on economy, efficiency and curbing government expenditures that the Bureau
of the Budget and the executive budget championed in
the mid-1920s probably succeeded as well as it did
because it was appropriate for the times. As one
source has observed, "'Normalcy', it was said, required the diminution of public activities."[25] In
this period during the 1920s when both political parties were interested in curbing government activities,
budget cutting became a popular course of action.

The next half century saw a greater and greater
executive centralization of budget activities coupled
with more and more legislative decentralization of
budget review. To make matters even more imbalanced
what attempts the legislative branch made in consolidating its budget review functions were usually ineffective.

The trends toward centralization of executive
budget activities and the decentralization of Congressional budget involvement can largely be attributed to
external crises and governmental reorganizations designed to meet world conditions. The "normalcy" of
the 1920s was shattered by the Great Depression of
1929. The Hoover Administration, however, was slow to
recognize the impact and seriousness of the economic
collapse.[26] Once it recognized the extent of the

-15-

economic problem, the administration's orthodox ideology limited its response to the crises to cutting "unnecessary" expenditures and struggling to achieve a balanced budget. The Roosevelt Administration changed much of this by embarking on what in terms of the 1930s was an ambitious recovery program on an emergency basis. However, the emergency situation tended to increase executive power at the expense of legislative control. Browne describes the effect on the appropriation process as follows:

> The Chief Executive was given unusual discretion..., especially as far as spending power was concerned. For the emergency Congress briefly surrendered the itemized appropriation act as a means of control over the vast sums appropriated for relief and recovery. In the case of some of the emergency appropriations the estimates for the expenditures were transmitted to Congress in special messages from the President and were not considered with the regular budget. These appropriations were frequently made in gross "for allocation by the President." In other words the appropriations were not made to the agencies but directly to the President. Although there were limitations on his spending he was not under close Congressional restraint.[27]

The crisis of the depression was overtaken in the 1940s by the crisis of World War II which in turn was overtaken by the crisis of the Cold War in the 1950s which was then overtaken by the perpetual crises of the 1960s and early 1970s. These multiple and continual crises resulted in Congress' granting more and more power and discretion to the President as the only central organ of the government capable of responding rapidly to meet real and perceived emergencies. Included in this grant of greater executive power was greater and greater executive discretion in the use of appropriations and the acceptance by Congress of executive interpretations of the world environment and what was best for the country.

It is difficult to overestimate the change the modern presidency has brought to the functioning of the US Government. In the context of the crises of the Great Depression the first major step in institution-

alizing the Presidency came as a result of the report
of the President's Committee on Administrative Management in 1937. The three committee members -- Louis
Brownlow, Charles Merriam and Luther Gulick -- had been
appointed by President Roosevelt to study the management powers and functions of the Office of the President and suggest means to improve it. The report recommended strengthening and improving the President's
personal staff, a recommendation FDR probably established the Committee to hear. The result was passage
of the Reorganization Act of 1939 under which Roosevelt reorganized his White House staff to be an effective Executive Office of the President. One of the
major reorganizational changes was the transfer of the
Bureau of the Budget from the Treasury Department into
the Executive Office. Similarly when Congress passed
the Full Employment Act of 1946 and established the
Council of Economic Advisers, this group was placed in
the Executive Office thereby further improving the
President's control of fiscal and budgetary matters.
The addition of such advisory bodies on a periodic or
permanent basis as the National Security Council, the
Domestic Council, Scientific Advisors and the Office
of Defense Mobilization has created an independent
source of expertise and capability in the White House
responsive to the President. The official bodies along
with an expansion in the number of personal advisers,
counselors and confidants to the President has finally
raised the specter of what Schlesinger has called "The
Imperial Presidency."

    While attempts of the executive branch to central-
ize operations have been largely successful, two note-
worthy attempts by Congress to reform its budgeting
functions met with failure. The first of these efforts
was the attempt to develop a legislative budget. A section of the Legislative Reorganization Act of 1946
provided for a Joint Committee on the Legislative Budget which was to develop a concurrent resolution early
in the legislative session establishing ceilings for
appropriations and expenditures for the coming fiscal
year. Since the resolution was to be binding on the
appropriation committees, it was anticipated that it
would increase Congressional control over the budgetary process. It simply did not work out this way. In
1947 the two houses passed differing resolutions which
a conference committee could not reconcile. The following year, while a resolution was passed by both houses,
the separate appropriations exceeded the self-imposed
budgetary ceiling by six billion dollars. In 1949 the

process was "deferred," never to be resurrected again for use. The second unsuccessful Congressional reform was the Omnibus appropriation bill. Following the failure of the Legislative budget the Chairman of the House Appropriations Committee indicated that for fiscal year 1951 the Committee would not review the agency appropriation requests on a piecemeal basis but rather would act on a single omnibus appropriation bill. True to its word the House passed a single bill in early May, a date which by 1950 standards was very late. By the time the Senate acted and a Conference Committee resolved the differences on the two versions of the act and the President signed the bill it was early September. Thus the Government had operated for over two months without any appropriations for the operation of agencies. The next year the House Committee on Appropriations, in opposition to its Chairman's wishes, voted against continuing the omnibus appropriations approach. Periodically the idea of an omnibus appropriations was resurfaced during the next twenty years but never with enough force to bring it to enactment.

Congress on several occasions established committees with more comprehensive budgetary-related functions in an attempt to gain a better perspective on fiscal affairs. A Joint Committee on Internal Revenue Taxation was established in 1926 and a House Committee on Executive Expenditures in 1927 along with its Senate counterpart in 1929 were formed. These latter two committees became the Committee on Government Operations, which still exist in both Houses today but exert little meaningful influence on the budget. In 1941 a novel approach was tried with the establishment of the Joint Committee on the Reduction of Nonessential Expenditures. The novel aspect of this committee was that it included, in addition to members of Congress, the Secretary of the Treasury and the Budget Director. In 1946 a Joint Economic Committee was formed pursuant to the Full Employment Act of that year. This Committee has done more to question the basic premises which underlie the annual budget submission than it has any other single function. Nevertheless this total effort has fallen far short of a comprehensive budget review.

As the budget grew in the 1950's and the 1960's the criticisms of Congress and its role in the budgetary process mounted. Writing in the mid 1960's, one widely quoted source in summarizing the many criticisms of Congressional budget performance noted that many observers felt the Congressional budgetary process was

irrational, that Congress had lost control of Federal
spending and that Congress lacked adequate information
to review the budget effectively.[28] Despite such broad-
side criticisms Congress did little to reform its budget review functions until it received that outside
impetus which has spurred many a Congressional action
-- a fight with the President.

When Republican President Richard Nixon took office in January 1969 he faced a Democratic-controlled
Congress that did not share many of his views on domestic social programs. What ensued was a running battle in which Nixon vetoed a number of appropriation
bills which called for more spending on domestic programs than the Administration believed the country
could or should afford. In addition Nixon's tendency
to blame Congress for excessive spending only added to
the controversy. However, it was probably the President's use of the device of impoundment that most
alienated Congress. Under existing anti-deficiency legislation impoundments were clearly authorized to provide for contingencies and to affect savings made possible by changes in requirements or those resulting
from greater efficiency of operations. The Nixon Administration extended the use of impoundment to include
aspects of fiscal policy as well as programmatic reasons. Thus funds were impounded on the grounds of
fighting inflation as well as "anticipation" -- that
Congress would revoke on-going programs because the
Administration had requested revocation. The scope of
the impoundment power was also extended by the sheer
volume of dollars involved. During his first four
years in office Nixon impounded approximately $40 bil-
lion.

In apparent retaliation Congress established a
Joint Committee in 1972 to study Congressional budget
practices. The Committee, which was chaired by Jamie
Whitten and Al Ullman, held hearings in 1973 and made
recommendations which were incorporated into a reform
bill. The bill was referred to the House Rules Committee which favorably reported it in November 1973. The
Rules Committee report noted that since the passage of
the Budget and Accounting Act of 1921 Congress had
done little to improve its "fiscal capabilities" and
had actually tended toward greater fragmentation in
budget making. The executive on the other hand according to the report had used his resources to achieve
"great concentration of program and financial policy-
making in his Executive Office." The report concluded

that this had resulted in "a dangerous mismatch in executive and legislative resources."[29] The report was
highly critical of Congressional budgetary practices
noting that there was really no Congressional budget
process but merely an "agglomeration of separate actions and decisions," and that this fragmentation had
made it difficult for Congress "to effectively assess
program priorities or to establish overall budget policy."[30] In recommending favorable action on the bill
the Committee report noted that the difficult task was
"to adopt the essential role of Congress in financial
matters to the profound changes that have penetrated
every facet of American Government."[31] Before adjourn-
ing for the year the House passed the reform bill by
a 386-23 vote. In the Senate the road to passage for
the bill was more complicated. The Committee on Government Operations favorably reported a bill that did not
include any provision dealing with impoundment. However, rather than act on the reported version of the
bill the Senate referred it to the Committee on Rules
and Administration two days after the House completed
action. The Rules and Administration Committee was directed to report a bill by February 1, 1974. After considerable behind the scenes negotiating a bill was reported in a revised version on March 6, 1974. The bill
passed the Senate by an 80-0 vote later that month.
Finally in June 1974 both Houses agreed to the version
that emerge from the Conference Committee.

As Public Law 93-344 was passed it provided for
significant changes in the Congressional budgetary process. The law changed the dates of the fiscal year in
the government from July 1 - June 30 to October 1 -
September 30. Since the President is still required to
submit his budget to Congress fifteen days after Congress convenes in January, this gives the Congress
three more months to review budget requests. In addition, by November 10 of the preceding year the executive
is required to submit a "current services budget" which
is merely the projected cost for the next fiscal year
of conducting current programs under existing policy.

Where the Budget and Accounting Act of 1921 created an executive agency (the Bureau of the Budget) to
assist the President, the Budget and Impoundment Control Act of 1974 created a Congressional Budget Office
to analyze budgetary data and material related to the
budget submission. The Act also created Budget Committees in each house. The House Committee has 23 members
and the Senate Committee fifteen. While the Senate
members are selected by normal procedural methods

relevant to all Committe assignments, the House Committee has five positions reserved for members of the Ways and Means Committee and five for Appropriations Committee members. Eleven members are from the eleven existing substantive legislative committees and one from the majority and one from the minority leaderships.

While the organizational changes were significant, the most important aspect of the bill is the manner in which it prescribes Congress to review the budget. The new procedure calls for a review of the President's budget submission by the budget committees who in turn by April 15 are to report concurrent resolutions to their respective bodies. By this date the budget committees will have performed necessary consultation with other involved committees and reviewed whatever analysis the Congressional Budget Office has made. The Congress is required to pass an initial resolution by May 15. This resolution is to establish budgetary targets according to the functional areas utilized in the President's budget. These areas include such categories as defense, health, income security, general government, agriculture and international affairs. The resolution includes any proposed tax changes or debt adjustments that will be required. The targets established in the first resolution are not binding but merely provide guidance to the other committees. In addition, all authorization bills are to be reported by May 15 so as to enable the various Appropriation Committees and subcommittees to perform their analyses. All appropriation bills are to be completed by no later than the seventh day after Labor Day. By September 15, Congress is to adopt a second resolution which will either agree with the targets established in the first resolution or if it does not agree, adjustments will have to be made to either appropriations, revenues or the debt limit. Final action on the budget is to be completed by September 30.

The bill also calls for placing so-called "backdoor spending" under closer Congressional supervision and requires both Houses of Congress to concur in any impoundment that terminates a program or reduces spending for fiscal policy reasons. A provision of the Antideficiency Act of 1950 which permitted the President not to spend funds as a result of "other developments" not further specified, was repealed.

The changes that Congress enacted which are designed to improve its budgetary review functions constitute a major step in restoring greater balance to the budgetary process. Nevertheless, the law places the burden on Congress to perform up to its own expectations and only time will tell if Congress is capable of meeting this challenge.

While the law was not to take effect until 1976, the Congressional leadership decided to implement part of it in 1975. Perhaps the major aspect of the law that was implemented called for the passage of the resolutions setting limits for total appropriations. This the Congress did when it passed the first resolution in May, as scheduled, and the second resolution on December 12, 1975. The date of passage of the second resolution was two months later than law required but nevertheless it passed. The final resolution was some $25 billion higher than President Ford requested. Overall, most sources felt the first year of the operation of the new system was successful. Congressional Quarterly observed that "...doubters misjudged the determination of key members of Congress to make the system work."[32]

The 1976 effort adhered to the schedule more closely. The passage of the first resolution in May and the second on September 16th marked the first full successful implementation of the legislation. In addition, opposition within the Congress to the new procedures was reduced as the legislators began to become accustomed to the new way of doing business.

If this attempt at reform eventually proves to be as unsuccessful as the Omnibus appropriations or the prior attempts at a legislative budget, then Congress may very well eliminate any pretext it maintains to the so-called "power of the purse." Dire predictions about the demise of legislative government are usually overstatements that underestimate the durability of representative bodies. This situation, however, may very well be the crossroads for representative government in American politics for it is difficult to conceive of the budgetary process becoming any less significant in terms of size and impact in the future. If the executive controls this process without a significant, rational contribution from the Congress, then we are likely to see the rising tide of opinion call for no contribution from Congress at all.

CHAPTER ONE

[1]Richard F. Fenno, Jr., The Power of the Purse
(Boston: Little, Brown and Company, 1966), p. XIII.

[2]A. E. Buck, The Budget in Governments of Today
(New York: The MacMillan Company, 1934), pp. 6-7.

[3]Jesse Burkhead, Government Budgeting (New York:
John Wiley and Sons, Inc., 1956), p. 3.

[4]Clinton Rossiter, Seedtime of the Republic (New
York: Harcourt, Brace and Company, 1953), p. 4.

[5]Rene Stourm, The Budget, translated by Thaddeus
Plazinski (New York: D. Appleton and Company, 1917),
p. 20.

[6]The Federalist, Modern Library edition (New York:
Random House, undated), p. 218.

[7]E. E. Naylor, The Federal Budget System in Operation (Washington: Privately Printed, 1941), p. 15.

[8]Lynton K. Caldwell, The Administrative Theories
of Hamilton and Jefferson (New York: Russell and
Russell, Inc., 1964), p. 214.

[9]This was actually the second budget under the
government of the Constitution. A budget for 1789 was
submitted to the House five months before the Treasury
Department was established. This budget had apparently
been prepared by a committee established for that purpose.

[10]Louis Fisher, President and Congress (New York:
The Free Press, 1972), p. 87.

[11]Buck, The Budget in Governments of Today, p. 38.

[12]Naylor, The Federal Budget System in Operation,
pp. 16-17.

[13]Fisher, President and Congress, p. 92.

[14]Ibid., p. 93.

[15]Robert D. Lee, Jr. and Ronald W. Johnson, Public
Budgeting Systems (Baltimore: Univ. Park Press, 1973) p. 7.

[16]Burkhead, _Government Budgeting,_ p. 17.

[17]Naylor, _The Federal Budget System in Operations_, p. 18.

[18]Burkhead, _Government Budgeting_, p. 19.

[19]U.S. Congress, House of Representatives, Select Committee on the Budget, _National Budget System_, Report No. 362, 66th Congress, 1st Session, October 8, 1919 (Washington: Government Printing Office, 1919), p. 4.

[20]_Ibid._

[21]_Ibid._, p. 5.

[22]_Ibid._, p. 7.

[23]U.S. Congress, Senate, Special Committee on the National Budget, _National Budget System_, Report No. 524, 66th Cong., 2d Session, April 13, 1920 (Washington: Government Printing Office, 1920), p. 1.

[24]Charles G. Dawes, _The First Year of the Budget of the United States_, (New York: Harper and Brothers, 1923) as cited in Naylor, _The Federal Budget System in Operation_, pp. 42-43.

[25]Vincent J. Browne, _The Control of the Public Budget_, (Washington: Public Affairs Press, 1949), p. 95.

[26]The Hoover Budget for Fiscal Year 1931 predicted a surplus for that year based on revenue estimates that later proved to be excessive.

[27]Browne, _The Control of the Public Budget_, p. 96.

[28]John S. Saloma III, _The Responsible Use of Power_ (Washington: American Enterprise Institute, 1964), pp. 27-32.

[29]U.S. Congress, House of Representatives, Committee on Rules, _Budget and Impoundment Control Act of 1973_, Report No. 93-658, 93rd Cong., 1st Sess., November 20, 1973 (Washington: Government Printing Office, 1973), p. 21.

[30]_Ibid._, pp. 21-22.

[31] _Ibid._, p. 20.

[32] "New Budget System Survives First Year Intact," _Congressional Quarterly Almanac_, XXXI, 916.

CHAPTER TWO

A Theoretical Perspective

A number of years ago David Easton defined theory as "...any kind of generalization or proposition that asserts that two or more things, activities or events covary under specified conditions."[1] In this broad definitional sense virtually every field of study would appear to be susceptible to, and benefit from having some type of theory or theories to explain its functioning. To be useful, a theory need not be comprehensive nor be an attempt to explain all aspects of a given subject. In fact cases of comprehensive theory are likely to be few and far between. The development of a particular theory is likely to depend primarily upon the state of knowledge in a given subject area in that the more we know about a subject the more likely we will be able to generalize about it in a meaningful sense. Budgeting as a field of study is no exception to this rule.

Budgeting as a function of government revolves around two basic questions. The first question is "How large should the budget be?" and the second is "How should the dollars in any budget be allocated among competing claims?" Any part that theory can play in answering or even helping to answer these two questions would be a vital contribution. However, as might be expected budgeting is rarely viewed from a purely theoretical perspective. In part this is due to the real world practical nature of budgeting. It also stems from the primitive state of American budgetary development prior to the passage of the Budget and

Accounting Act of 1921. Since we did not really have a comprehensive budgetary system until then it would have been unrealistic to expect early scholars of public administration to have concerned themselves with such abstract matters. In addition, once a budget system was installed the major concerns for the next two decades were with evaluating its functioning and insuring its perpetuation. This called for what Rowland Egger referred to over thirty years ago as "...a fundamental reorientation of our thinking about the budget function."[2] As a result our concern with "budgetary theory" has been a rather recent phenomenon.

In a landmark article published at the end of 1940, V. O. Key raised the issue that basically reflected the fundamental reorientation that Egger said was needed. Key noted that "On the most significant aspect of public budgeting, i.e., the allocation of expenditures among different purposes so as to achieve the greatest return, American budgetary literature is singularly arid."[3] In this article Key bemoaned what he referred to as a lack of budgetary theory. In the end however Key observed that, "It is not to be concluded that by excogitation a set of principles may be formulated on the basis of which the harassed budget official may devise an automatic technique for the allocation of financial resources."[4] While this conclusion is fairly obvious it did need stating since it implied that while there were still no overall accepted budgetary principles governing the allocation of resources, there were other areas for study that would be of assistance to the "harassed budget official." Key suggested the budgetary process, the role of legislatures, and decision-making analysis as fruitful areas for further study.

The work of many scholars who followed Key did indeed focus on other aspects of budgetary interest rather than searching for a purely theoretical basis upon which to reach allocative decisions. The reason for this is quite simple. There is no single theoretical answer to the complex questions that are embodied in any budget. As a result, the attempts to develop a more mundane working theory of budgeting have focused on four basic approaches. These approaches have been (1) procedural and technical (2) economic analysis (3) approaches to decision-making theory and (4) quantitative techniques. The four approaches in practice are not necessarily exclusive and in fact have a considerable area of overlap. They are offered here primarily as a means of categorizing where "budgetary theory" has developed and in what manner.

Procedural and Technical Approaches

The first procedural post-1921 reform to budgeting that gained widespread support was the movement toward "performance budgeting." Briefly, a performance budget focuses on those things and activities that government performs i.e., ends in relation to some measure of output. The traditional budget places its main focus on what government buys, so-called elements of expense: personnel services, travel, supplies, equipment, utilities. The stress in the traditional budget is on the input of funds rather than the output of what the funds achieve. The performance budget stresses the ends for which the services are procured: to have safe, clean streets; to achieve an effective road system. The main emphasis shifts to the output. These end-objectives or outputs are measured against agreed-upon performance standards such as the number of tons of garbage collected or the number of miles of roads paved. In this manner the performance of governmental units can be compared on a year by year basis and requests for budgetary adjustments can be analyzed in this light. All sorts of comparisons can be made with the resulting data.

The earliest experimentation with performance budgeting was at the municipal level in New York City prior to World War I. The impact of this experiment, however, was slight. It was the Hoover Commission recommendation in 1949 that the government adopt the performance budget that brought about its initial wide-spread popular acceptance. The hold that the concept of performance budgeting had on leaders in the field of public administration thought at that time is apparent in the report of the "Symposium on Budget Theory" that was held in 1949 and attended by many well known authorities on budgeting. The report noted at that time, "The most discussed single concept in current budget thinking is the performance budget." The conferees concluded that the performance budget rested upon "sound experience" and was "administratively and politically feasible."[5] Some government agencies responding to the Hoover Commission recommendations adopted performance budgets during this period. The Defense Department and its various components probably can be considered to have led the way, since amendments to the

National Security Act in 1949 called for the military
to adopt performance budgeting. Similarly, scattered
municipalities throughout the country adopted performance budgets. Overall, however, performance budgeting
turned out not to be the cure-all it was expected to
be. Although the Budget and Accounting Procedures Act
of 1950 provided a legislative impetus for all governmental agencies to adopt performance budgets, not many
agencies ever did. One likely reason for its lack of
success throughout the government is that performance
measurement primarily lends itself to areas where
repetitive, measurable workload data can be developed
and is useful in gauging relative merit. Unfortunately,
assuming workload data can be gathered, workload data
alone is not necessarily useful to decide on whether or
not an activity should be done at all, the basic
utility of a program once it is decided to be done, or
how it compares in terms of economy, efficiency, and
performance to other programs. It is least useful in
determining if a governmental operation is achieving
its objectives. Performance budgeting as a result has
been useful only in limited areas. In any respect it
represents an advance over strictly traditional budgeting by element of expense.

Another procedural technique offered was the
"alternative budget system." In the words of its chief
proponent Verne B. Lewis:

Under this procedure, each administrative
official who prepares a budget estimate,
either as a basis for an appropriation
request or an allotment request after the
appropriation is made, would be required to
prepare a basic budget estimate supplemented
by skeleton plans for alternative amounts.
If the amount of the basic estimate equals
100, the alternatives might represent,
respectively, 80, 90, 110 and 120 percent
of that amount. The number of alternatives
might vary with the situation.[6]

Lewis' proposal had the merit of focusing on
limited adjustments and presenting various alternatives
to spending levels since these are really the main
focus of budget preparation. In other words the focus
is on the proper place. His approach also utilized the
analytical capabilities of the many echelons of a
government agency. Incremental analysis of the depth
that Lewis' proposal envisioned could only be performed
by the numerous agency budget analysts. The idea of

involving individual analysts was designed to provide detailed technical expertise to the decision-maker, who in-turn could then weigh the technical, political and practical aspects of the problem. The basic short-comings of the suggestion are the magnitude of the work involved and the failure of the system to address the basic question of whether the program should be done at all. Selecting the 90% alternative of something that need not be done at all would be no real accomplishment. What use has been made of the alternative budget method has primarily been within government agencies in the preparation stage of their budgets. Agencies have been reluctant to offer such alternative programs to sources outside their own departments for fear that alternatives reflect lower degrees of acceptability, hence reduced budgets.

The last major procedural reform attempted by the Federal government was the adoption of the Planning-Programing-Budgeting System (PPBS) during the 1960s. The system was initiated in the Defense Department in 1961 by Secretary of Defense, Robert McNamara and his Comptroller Charles Hitch. Since its inception so much has been written about PPBS that it is almost impossible to provide anything resembling a brief presentation of its characteristics, strengths, and shortcomings.

In brief the basic idea of PPBS was to integrate the functions of planning, programing, and budgeting into a comprehensive, interrelated system for decision-making relating to resource allocation. These functions as performed until that time in the Defense Department were separate activities encompassing different groups of people and different periods of time. As an example, planning which was largely a military function, varied in its time span from short-range (1-3 Years), to mid-range (3-5 Years) to long-range (5-10 Years). However, there were rarely any attempts to relate dollar costs to the specific plans. As a result plans could be developed, staffed, and approved which would have been so costly to implement that they were really impractical from a budgetary standpoint. As an example, the Army plans could be based on the premise that twenty divisions were re-quired for the Army to perform its mission. In the face of budgetary constraints as they existed in the late 1950's, the concept of twenty divisions repre-sented more of a wish than a reality. From such a standpoint the plan as a proposed course of action was useless because its cost far exceeded any budgetary capability to finance and any political willingness to support. Similarly, since budgeting which was performed primarily by civilians in the department usually concerned itself with only one year at a time, the multi-year impact of current decisions was almost impossible to identify. As competing weapons systems decisions began to take on more long term aspects, from research and development to deployment, total life cycle costs became vital to the decision-maker in helping determine which system was most cost effective. A one year budget total in such cases considered in isolation concealed more than it told. In fact in some cases low initial-year costs as reflected in a single year budget distorted rational decision-making because full life cycle funding, if displayed, would have demonstrated that the succeeding years raised the overall price tag on a weapon to a point where it might not have been selected as a feasible option.

A third major shortcoming in the pre-PPBS resource allocation process in the Defense Department dealt with mission objectives and departmental budgeting. Each of the military departments planned and budgeted to perform its roles and missions as it independently interpreted them. As a result the Army could base its mission accomplishment on the availability of the Air Force having a capability to move a significant number of Army combat troops from one point to another in a given span of time. On the other hand, the Air Force would decide how many transport planes it needed by evaluating requirements for all types of planes against all the missions it was assigned. The Army requirement for Air Force support and the Air Force determination of what part of its resources it could allocate to support for the Army usually did not coincide. The Army then could be in the position where it was depending upon a non-existent or at least limited Air Force capability to move Army troops to perform the Army mission. Since resources were allocated to the military departments based on their own individual interpretations of priorities and missions, what emerged was not a comprehensive integrated national security policy but rather three departmental security policies based on single service views.

PPBS attempted to solve these three major deficiencies. In order to relate planning to the budget process, PPBS required that cost annexes be attached to all plans. The objective was to eliminate the "pie in the sky" concept in planning. Planners were required to face the price tag portion of their proposed endeavors and evaluate the extent to which plans and resources were in correlation. To overcome the one year limitation in budgeting, multi-year programing was implemented. The particular structure in the Defense Department was called the Five Year Defense Plan (FYDP) but by any name it was an attempt to evaluate costs over an extended period of time. The FYDP was actually an 8 year display that showed the last full year, the current year of budget execution, the next budget year and five so-called "outyears." In order to develop more rational resource allocations, a program structure was established which focused on specific missions and cut across military service lines. As an example, a program was established for Strategic Forces.

In this program the resources for such things as Air Force Intercontinental Ballistic Missiles(ICBM) and the Navy POLARIS submarine system were evaluated. By combining weapons with a view toward what mission they accomplished, regardless of what military department operated them, comparisons could be made as to how much of any particular weapon was needed to accomplish an overall mission. Forces and equipment were related to mission rather than to competing claims within a particular military department. During the 1961-65 period PPBS worked so well in the Defense Department that President Johnson attempted to extend it to the entire Federal bureaucracy in 1965.

As a complete system for resource allocation PPBS continued to function in the Defense Department, but it never really was effective in the non-defense sector. There were limited exceptions to this statement but as a rule it stands true. The Nixon Administration began downplaying PPBS soon after it took office and by the end of Nixon's first term, PPBS could be considered to have died in the non-defense area. There were few mourners at its demise. Some remnants of PPBS still survive even in those agencies where it was least effective and least appreciated. However, as a comprehensive system it is no more.

The obvious question is why did the PPBS system work in the Defense area but not in other areas. Certainly it is true that the Defense Department was much further advanced in its planning function than other civilian agencies. A full set of plans was

reviewed and evaluated annually in the Department. A
full scale planning cycle can be said to have existed
prior to 1961. In addition, the military departments
had experience with program budgeting. At the time of
the installation of PPBS, the Army and Air Force were
using program structures not too unlike those established by the Secretary of Defense to reach their own
allocation decisions. However, when all is said and
done the most likely reason for the difference in
success is related to the state of knowledge. We
simply know how to make war better than we know how to
employ the hard-core unemployed, educate the otherwise
uneducatable and in general alter asocial and anti-
social behavior. The number of missiles, bombers and
troops needed to cope with a finite number of enemies
who are assumed to have certain military capabilities
is a calculable problem. Defense analysts simply know
how to do what they are asked regardless of the com-
plexity. The same is not true of social programs.
Programs such as HEAD START are initiated by Congressional action and assigned to an executive department.
Yet we still have no evidence or experience that what
the program attempts to accomplish can actually be
done at all, let alone by the method proposed. The
state of knowledge in the social programs area is
usually primitive and what is being attempted is often
subject to disagreement. Without agreed upon objectives,
a concerted effort with purpose is unlikely. Analysis
of any type regardless of its sophistication cannot and
will not change this. PPBS simply assumed a unity of
purpose, state of knowledge and capability to influence
outcomes that did not exist in the civilian programs of
the government. Perhaps they should not exist to the
extent that they do in military areas. Nevertheless
if such is the case then overselling PPBS as a cure-
all contributed little to long term budgetary development.

In retrospect PPBS had one thing in common with
prior budgetary reform. It was not really the drastic
reform to governmental budgeting that it originally was
expected to be. It simply did not provide the mechanism to answer all the major budgetary questions that
exist and remain unsolved. It was probably unrealistic
to expect that it would. As one source observed, "The
PPB system that is being developed portends a radical
change in the central function of budgeting, but it is
anchored to half a century of tradition and evaluation."[7] The half century of tradition included such
widely accepted practices as program and performance

budgeting concepts, and program analysis as well as a variety of nonbudgetary practices. Lee and Johnson refer to the latter as "nonbudgetary antecedents to PPB" and include such things as operations research, economic analysis, general systems theory, cybernetics, computer hardware and systems analysis.[8] In the end it may not be the mechanical techniques and procedures of PPBS that have the lasting effects but rather the development of a way of looking and thinking about the purpose and objectives of government programs that has the most impact. PPBS required objectives to be developed and clarified to an extent not previously achieved. If nothing else this is a beginning for if we did not have the basic concepts embodied in PPBS we would surely have to go out and invent them.

Economic Analysis

The budget officer in a government agency is faced with the problem of allocating scarce resources among competing claims in a manner that will satisfy a variety of constituents and claimants. His problem is basically one of allocation. The business manager similarly has a problem in deciding how to allocate his available resources in order to maximize his goals or the goals of his firm. The business manager, however, has two decided advantages in reaching his allocative decisions. He knows in advance that the dominant goal he seeks to achieve in the long run is the maximization of profit and he has the impersonal forces of the market to use as a guide. Armed with these two elements, the business manager is prepared to face the world and his competition. The public official does not have any such widely agreed upon standards to guide his conduct. His goals are often unclear and he often has no way to know if he has achieved them. It is not surprising then that the writers dealing with the problem of public expenditures and budget officers themselves should turn longingly as have business managers to the field of economics in the hope that some help would be forthcoming.

One of the first economic ideas that found some acceptability as a guide to public expenditure policy is that of marginal utility. Marginal utility theory as a contribution to economic thought did not appear until the latter part of the 19th century. Three Austria economists, Carl Menger, Friedrich Von Weiser and Eugen Von Bohm-Bawerk, and an Englishman William

Stanley Jevons were the major exponents of this revolutionary new way of viewing and measuring value. The
basic idea of marginal utility is that the value of any
given unit of a commodity is determined by the value of
the last increment of that commodity added to the
existing level. In an economic sense this made utility
totally subjective and determined by both exchange and
distribution and explained price in the market on the
basis of utility rather than costs of production. The
marginal utility theorists were advocates of pure
rationality, economic man and free competition. Nevertheless they were able to see the applicability of
their ideas to governmental policy. According to Von
Weiser, "To this extent the plan of state economy where
it is determined by aggregate valuations is controlled
precisely like the economy which computes according to
partial value and desires to extend the margin of use
as far as possible."[9] In theoretical terms the state
increases total social benefits by applying the concept of marginal utility as a guide to its decision-
making.

It was really the concept of marginal utility that
Pigou was expounding when he made his oft-quoted observation concerning the need for government to insure
that the last dollar it spent on battleships provided
as much utility to the society as the last dollar spent
on poor relief. The problem, of course, and Pigou was
certainly aware of it, is how to measure and compare
the utility derived from such diverse fields as defense
and welfare. The question remains what type of value
can be assigned to these areas as aggregates and how
do you measure each additional increment. The answer
is that it cannot scientifically be done. Generally,
we have been willing to leave the matter to be
determined by the political process rather than rely on
objective analysis. Overall, however, it is as Key
observed that applying marginal utility analysis to
public expenditures lacks a certain degree of reality.
Nevertheless, as a manner of thinking about expenditure
proposals and planning spending programs, marginal
utility provides an excellent frame of reference or
perspective by which to view program size and program
successes.

Cost/benefit analysis attempts to overcome certain
of the "lack of reality" problems that the classical
theory of marginal utility faces and in effect tries
to apply the basic theory to existing cases. In a
definitional sense cost/benefit analysis is merely the

-36-

attempt to make systematic and rational calculations of the cost of any government endeavor in relation to its benefits. It attempts to answer the question "what do we get in return for what we spend?" The relationship between the two is the key aspect. Usually the technique is most effective in relating alternative methods of achieving an agreed upon goal. Cost/benefit analysis will not determine goals but rather it attempts to determine the economically "best" method of goal accomplishment. Just as the marginal utility economists relied on rationality, economic man and competition, so the cost/benefit analyst assumed that his evaluation will be basically rational. He will expect that considerations similar to those that govern economic decisions in the market will prevail and that competitive choices and allocations can be accomplished.

There are several obvious problems involved in conducting cost/benefit analysis even if one assumes that the analyst is perceptive enough to be aware of all possible alternatives in any given situation. The problems basically relate to the two elements in the equation -- cost and benefit. Dollar costs in a budget are relatively easy to identify but unfortunately dollar costs are often inadequate to express the totality of social issues. If the cost involves the issue of human lives, how does the rational analyst assign a value to a life? Certain economic calculations can determine earning power and future life expectancy but a humane society probably requires more than this. Similarly, indirect costs cannot always be captured. What is the true cost of polluted streams and defaced landscapes? This is further complicated by the subjectivity of costs of this type. Again, economic values can be attached to such losses but no rational person contends that the loss is purely economic. The same point can be made for benefits. Capturing all the benefits of any given government program is unlikely. In fact, some analysts believe that the citizens tend to downgrade the benefits they receive from government action often because the benefits are long term and we tend to value immediate benefits more than future benefits.[10] In addition benefits can be intangible just as costs often are. What is the benefit to a taxpayer of the education of his neighbors children? Overall, to conduct an appropriate cost/benefit analysis an amount of information and state of knowledge far beyond what we usually have is required. However, to their advantage many analysts do indicate that certain stated assumptions have to be made about aspects of any analysis. As long as these assumptions are made clear and offered for acceptance or rejection by the decision-maker then the results can be viewed as useful in that more limited context. From most standpoints at least if assumptions are explicit, this represents an advance over analysis that tends to be based on unstated assumptions which cannot be verified by an outside observer.

In an overall sense if the elements of costs and benefits for all government programs could be identified government should conduct those programs that will produce the most favorable ratio of benefit to cost. On an operational level for a budget officer cost/benefit analysis at least provides a tool for attempting to determine which of several ways will be the most economically efficient manner of achieving an objective. Again, the assumption is that if all things are equal, the "best" choice will be apparent but then rarely are all things equal.

Another aspect of economics that has attracted the interest of financial managers in the government service is that of public goods and market imperfection. In this sense the concept of public goods is best understood in relation to its opposite number, private goods. Private goods are those goods which have certain characteristics, such as divisibility in that the good can be used by an individual and one individual alone with a relatively low cost to exclude anyone else from using the good. A pair of shoes is a typical example. The use of a single pair of shoes by one person obviously excludes everyone else from using the shoes at the same time. In addition, the cost and benefits of private goods can be determined especially since there are usually few externalities involved, i.e., third parties who were not party to the transaction are rarely involved. Pure private goods are regulated by the market as a means of determining production and consumption levels. Public goods on the other hand are usually not divisible, cannot exclude enjoyment of benefits by those who do not pay for them, have significant external effects, and have costs and benefits which are very difficult to compute. The classic example of a public good is national defense. In the case of such goods and services the market is a highly unreliable guide as to how much of a given good should be provided to society. In fact, the market could be expected to fail to operate in the public interest or would not achieve an efficient allocation of society's resources. What then is the answer to the allocation of public goods question? One useful concept which embodies ideas of marginal utility, cost/benefit analysis and welfare economics is that of maximum social gain. This basic principle maintains that the societal allocation for public goods or the total spending by the public sector should be extended in each area and in the aggregate until the marginal social value of the next dollar spent equals the marginal social cost. If there is a choice of alternatives to select, the alternative method which gives society the largest benefit in relation to cost should be selected. Concepts of social cost and social gain, however, have two basic aspects. One is efficiency and is relatively easy to understand. Efficiency is simply measured by the value of what is given up for what is gained. The second aspect is that of equity. Equity, however, necessitates an ethical judgment. There is no way to prove logically or empirically that taking tax money from the rich and providing the poor with social services creates more utility for society. Nevertheless, we accept this concept of welfare economics and its serves as a fundamental part of our political system. The political concept embodied in this idea is that to maximize social utility in any society, income should be shifted from those individuals for whom additional income has low social utility to those for whom additional income would have a high social utility.[11] These shifts should continue until the marginal social utility of income is equal for all people.

This principle, therefore, provides a theoretical answer to the following questions. How much should government spend? The government should spend until the amount of social utility produced equates to the social disutility of taxes taken from the private sector. What should government spend its money for and how much? Government should spend among the various programs so that the social utility derived from each program equals the social utility derived from all other programs. What kind of taxes should government collect and how much? Government should tax so that social disutility of the last dollar raised from each kind of tax should equal social disutility of every other type of tax.

The end result of this type of analysis is that governmental decision-makers attempt to maximize the return to society in terms of total social benefits derived. Obviously every individual has a different concept of utility and value. One man treasures gold,

another favors music. Nevertheless by making the
assumption that every one has an equal set of value preferences, social policies can be viewed as striving for
"Pareto optimality." This situation is achieved when
any change in society improves the condition of at least
one person while not harming any person. One can hard-
ly argue with such an approach but few cases in the
world are this clear.

The use of economic analysis in budgeting is primarily of benefit as a way of looking at things. It is
a mind set that stresses rationality and attempts to
perceive allocational decisions in that context. The
only danger involved in this perspective is that it
occasionally tends to neglect all other aspects --
particularly the political -- from consideration. This
undoubtedly dooms the approach to failure. Only when
it is blended with political consideration is economic
analysis likely to be useful to budget officers.

Decision-Making Analysis

Another area of interest to financial managers is
that of the process of decision-making. Financial
managers continually face the problem of how to make
decisions which result in the most favorable outcomes.
Regardless of the nature of the budget structure itself and economic factors involved, the manager still
must make a choice and choice is the basic ingredient
of decision-making.

In general, there are three basic models of
decision-making. The first is what has been called the
rational comprehensive model of decision-making. This
model depicts the way we were all taught in our earliest school days that all decisions were made. The
rational comprehensive model in reality embodies the
scientific method. It starts on the assumption that a
problem is recognized. In deciding to solve the problem, the decision-maker attempts to gather all the
pertinent facts about the situation. The decision-
maker then analyzes all of the facts that he has gathered and develops all the feasible alternatives to re-
solve the problem. He then analyzes the alternatives
and selects the best one. He applies this best
alternative and solves the problem. This model has
several significant unstated assumptions underlying it.
Among these assumptions are that all the pertinent facts
can be gathered; these facts can be gathered at little

or no cost to the decision-maker and certainly the facts must be gathered within the time period necessary to face the problem; that an individual decision-maker can absorb all the relevant facts and understand them; that he can view all the facts objectively; that he knows all the possible alternatives; that he can recognize the <u>best</u> alternative; and that his selection solves the problem. There is reason to question that all these conditions are present except in the simplest of cases. It is difficult to think of a case where these conditions are all met.

In budgetary terms, PPBS was the closest attempt to build a decision-making structure based on a rational comprehensive model. PPBS assumed all or almost all the above factors were present and could be accomplished by rational men. The failure of PPBS might in part be attributed to this very aspect. Applied to areas where all the factors for the rational comprehensive model were present, PPBS would work. Applying PPBS to areas where the factors were not present could only lead to frustration and failure.

At the other end of the spectrum from the rational comprehensive model is the incrementalist model.

The classical statement of the incrementalist model was made by Charles Lindblom and its major advocate in the budgetary area is Aaron Wildavsky. Lindblom's analysis starts from the premise that because the rational comprehensive model is applicable only to relatively simple problems it is of little value to the decision-maker in his day to day functioning. What Lindblom is searching for is a model that will help the decision-maker in the real world to "muddle through."[12] To achieve this the decision-maker is forced to make a series of successive limited comparisons which do not require distinctions between means and ends and do not require agreement on fundamental objectives or values. As a result evaluation and empirical evidence are intertwined and the main attention is directed to marginal or incremental changes to the existing situation. In the end, the policy that emerges is "good" because there has been agreement on that policy by all interested participants. The decision-maker is open to inputs from partisans in the political process. The partisans eventually accommodate each other by mutual adjustment. A major advantage of the incremental decision-making process is that it avoids serious mistakes because new policy so closely resembles old policy and the change is, in the last analysis, reversible or increaseable in the same direction. Because policy change is based on previous policy it is basically rational, for what can be more rational than what we are now doing. The incremental model acknowledges that the decision-maker is not all knowing and wise.

Wildavsky in his famous The Politics of the Budgetary Process stresses how budget changes are incremental adjustments to a previous base. This embodies both aspects of Lindblom's model in that the base (previous decisions) is rational and future policy directions are merely incremental adjustments to the base. As Schick says this approach makes it "...possible to quarantine budget conflict to the increment that deals with proposed program additions."[13] This leads budget officials, according to Wildavsky, to reach not for a final solution that is merely an improvement over the present situation. Herbert Simon's term "Satisfice" is the best one-word explanation of the decision-makers' objective.

The criticisms of the incrementalist model are that on some occasions more than merely incremental changes are needed and not every case of mutual adjustment considers all the affected interests equally. Witness the attempts of the Congress to "Satisfice" over the issue of slavery before the Civil War. The incremental adjustments primarily focused on the entry of states into the Union. To maintain the balance in the Senate care was taken to insure that each new slave state that entered the Union was balanced by a free state. These incremental adjustments merely deferred looking at slavery as a moral question, which eventually was solved only by a war. In the end the political system through mutual adjustment failed. The separation of means and ends simply failed to work. In addition the mutual adjustment process excluded one very vital group from the process of accommodation -- the slaves themselves. Overall the incremental model tends to be too short ranged in conception and places too much emphasis on the process of decision-making itself to the detriment of policy-making outcomes. Good policy is not always what we can merely agree upon for we can all agree to be wrong.

Between these two extremes are various models that blend elements of both. Etzioni's mixed scanning model is a good example of such an approach. In this case the decision-maker extends a certain amount of his effort to scanning the horizon for danger signals and long range implications of his decisions as well as short term effects. The analogy of the chess player is most applicable. The player explores several strategies in varying degrees and then implements his choice on an incremental basis -- one move at a time. This tends to force something more than consideration of merely short term, immediate factors in reaching a decision. According to Etzioni, "Scanning ...combines the collection, processing and evaluation of information with the process of making choices."[14]

Our social security system is a good example of where the mixed scanning concept could be applicable. Since its passage in the early days of the New Deal, the adjustments to the basic social security law have tended to be incremental in that the amount of old age benefits that is paid has been increased periodically by a fixed amount as has the tax rate and tax base. Little attention has been paid to where this would all lead in terms of the ability of the social security trust fund to maintain itself in 50 or 100 years. Under a mixed scanning concept both the short term incremental change would be made, but evaluations of the long term fundamental impact would be presented to the decision-maker. Such long term factors might force a reconsideration of how the fund is financed in the future. This type of a decision would be more than an incremental one. It would be a fundamental decision which would set the stage for many incremental follow-on decisions.

As Wildavsky says, most budget decisions are made utilizing the incremental model. This has resulted over the years in an ever growing budget which tends to add programs without ever examining the on-going programs adequately. In a period of economic expansion such a course of action is not necessarily a major problem. New programs are added from the additional taxes that come from economic growth. Economic stagnation, however, tends to dry up any new source of revenue and forces some other approach to the problem.

Quantitative Factors

A fourth area of consideration is that of the application of more and more quantitative considerations into budgeting. If there is a current rule of thumb in budgeting which has permeated budget techniques from performance budgeting to PPBS, it is wherever possible quantify. Quantification, however, has also been used as an explanation of the functioning of the budgetary process. Wildavsky and his associates in 1966 developed a theoretical approach to budgeting that emphasized the "...striking regularities in the budgetary process."[15] This approach focused on a series of equations to summarize budgetary outcomes. Such an approach was consistent with Wildavsky's previous work and was merely an attempt to depict in quantitative terms how outcomes could be anticipated because roles and expectations of the participants in the process were relatively constant. It is not surprising that if the same actors, did the same things and had the same expectations from year to year, that outcomes could be quite predictable. Wildavsky et al used the slight or marginal differences in agency yearly budgets to depict how little things changed. This led to the conclusion that "...up to a random error of reasonable magnitude, the budgetary process of the United States government is equivalent to a set of temporally stable linear decision rules."[16]

These findings were challenged by Natchez and Bupp who maintained that despite what appeared to be a relatively constant or predictable growth levels of appropriations, a great deal of programmatic shifting occurred within the budgetary levels.[17] The Natchez and Bupp contention was that merely because an agency's appropriation grew from X to X+10 over a given period of time, it did not mean that the agency was doing the same thing with the X dollars. Shifting agency priorities and areas of interest tended to complicate the matter. The Natchez and Bupp explanation downplayed the "constancy" in the budgetary process and emphasized the programmatic output that varied within what appeared to be predictable growth in budget figures. This is especially evident in budgeting for fixed costs. As the costs of things such as utilities increased, agencies have been required to shift a greater portion of their operating costs to meet this increase. Not all increases of this type are susceptible to adding to the budget because they occur during the execution phase of the budget when appropriations have already been determined.

Depending on where one places the primary emphasis both quantified approaches have merit. The Wildavsky approach again tends to emphasize the process of budgeting while the Natchez and Bupp focus on outcomes.

Both approaches point out the utility of quantitative approaches to understanding budgetary actions, outcomes and trends.

It is into this historical setting and theoretical perspective that zero-base budgeting enters the scene. From the outset it should be understood that zero-base budgeting is not a totally new concept divorced from what has come before it. In fact it is built upon much that has come before it. This thought should be of comfort to those individuals throughout the public sector who are called upon to develop zero-base budgets. In reality the ability of budgeteers to understand that they already possess many of the skills needed to prepare a zero-base budget should contribute to whatever success the concept has in the public sector.

FOOTNOTES

CHAPTER TWO

[1] David Easton, _A Systems Analysis of Political Life_ (New York: John Wiley & Sons, 1965), p.7.

[2] Rowland Egger, "Power is Not Enough," _State Government_ (August, 1940) reprinted in Catheryn Seckler - Hudson, _Budgeting: An Instrument of Planning and Management_ (Washington: The American University, 1944), p. 67.

[3] V.O. Key, "The Lack of a Budgetary Theory," _American Political Science Review_, XXXIV (December, 1940), 1137.

[4] _Ibid._, 1143.

[5] "Symposium on Budget Theory," _Public Administration Review_, XII (Winter, 1952), 49.

[6] Verne B. Lewis, "Toward a Theory of Budgeting," _Public Administration Review_, XII (Winter, 1952), 49.

[7] Allen Schick, "The Road to PPB: The Stages of Budget Reform," _Public Administration Review_, XXVI (December, 1966), 243.

[8] Robert D. Lee, Jr. and Ronald W. Johnson, _Public Budgeting Systems_ (Baltimore: Univ. Park Press, 1973), pp. 116-17.

[9] Frederick von Weiser, _Social Economics_, excerpts reprinted in _Source Readings in Economic Thought_, edited by Philip C. Newman, Arthur D. Gayer and Milton H. Spencer (New York: W.W. Norton Co., Inc., 1954), p.389.

[10] As an example, see Anthony Downs, "Why the Government Budget is Too Small in a Democracy," _World Politics_, XII (1960), 541-63.

[11] For an excellent but not too complex evaluation of the principles of welfare economics reflected by this statement see Ben B. Seligman, _Currents in Modern_

Economics (New York: The Free Press of Glencoe, 1963), pp. 477-96.

[12]Charles E. Lindblom, "The Science of 'Muddling Through'," Public Administration Review, XIX (Spring, 1959), 79-88.

[13]Allen Schick, "The Battle of the Budget" in Congress Against the President, edited by Harvey C. Mansfield, Sr. (New York: Praeger Publishers, 1975), p.57.

[14]Amitai Etzioni, The Active Society (New York: The Free Press, 1968),p. 286. Chapter 12 of this work provides a comprehensive explanation of the mixed scanning model.

[15]Otto A. Davis, M.A.H. Dempster and Aaron Wildavsky, "A Theory of the Budgetary Process," American Political Science Review, LX (September, 1966), 529.

[16]Ibid., 537.

[17]Peter B. Natchez and Irvin C. Bupp, "Policy and Priority in the Budgetary Process," American Political Science Review, LXVII (September, 1973), 951-63.

CHAPTER THREE

WHERE ZBB FITS -- THEORY AND PRACTICE

THEORY

It is commonly asserted that Zero-Base Budgeting means justifying everything "from the ground up," from a "zero-base," from "scratch." That's fine. Unfortunately the definition is the easy part; the implementation of how this is to be done -- and the assessment that such a process will provide for a more rational allocation of resources -- is the real question.

The problem in implementation stems from a basic disagreement between theorists and practitioners of budgeting (on both sides) concerning how public resource allocation decisions are made and whether _formalized_, budgetary systems can aid in making better or more rational decisions. The heart of this disagreement goes to differing perceptions of the ability of man to incorporate the proper amount of information that will aid in decision-making, and perhaps more importantly, of the wisdom of implementing systems which attempt to incorporate this ability. As one observer has commented,

> [T]he development of budgetary procedures
> and methods is characterized by the attempt
> to make up for a perceived deficiency of
> the right amounts of the right kinds of
> information needed in the process of re-
> source allocation...[E]very change that has
> been recommended for improving budgetary

procedures has eventually been assessed...
on the grounds of implicitly or explicitly
held conceptions about the extent to which
it is possible for the decision making process to be responsive to new inputs of information.[1]

While the distinctions may be overdrawn for the
sake of illustration, we can delineate arguments from
two basic positions in this debate: those espousing a
"muddling through" or incremental approach to budgeting,
and those advocating a comprehensive method.

As we noted in an earlier discussion, the comprehensive approach assumes that the goals and objectives
of each major area of government activity can be identified and examined. As Charles Schultze, Director of
the Bureau of the Budget under President Johnson, has
said, such an approach "attempts to force government
agencies to step back and reflect on the fundamental
aims of their current programs."[2] Once these goals and
objectives are established, possible alternatives toward achievement are set forth, which in turn are examined under cost/benefit and cost/effectiveness analysis. When such analysis is completed, and considered
in light of available resources, then the effectiveness
of government expenditures can be increased so as to
enhance societal needs. The process is an iterative
one whereby "we discover our values while considering
the means to achieve them, and [the fact] that values
are hierarchical in nature results in a continual change
and evolution of our objectives."[3] Heavy emphasis is
placed on marginal analysis where the worth of an additional dollar invested in one program is weighed
against the benefits of additional dollars invested in
other programs. In recent years the approach has come
to be identified most with "program budgeting," and
attempts to address what V.O. Key, thirty-five years
ago, viewed as "the basic budgeting problem...: On
what basis should it be decided to allocate x dollars
to activity A instead of activity B?"[4]

Perhaps the most optimistic expression of what
such an approach was designed to accomplish can be seen
from President Johnson's comments at a press conference
in August 1965, when he introduced the PPB System, the
formalized and systematic budget method that implemented program budgeting throughout the Executive Branch
after the claimed successful Department of Defense experience. His words deserve to be quoted in extenso:

I have just concluded a meeting with the
Cabinet and with the heads of Federal
agencies, and I am asking each of them to
immediately begin to introduce a very new
and very revolutionary system of planning
and budgeting throughout the vast Federal
Government, so that through the tools of
modern management the full promise of a
finer life can be brought to every American
at the lowest possible cost.

Under this new system each Cabinet and
agency head will set up a very special
staff of experts who, using the most modern
methods of program analysis, will define
the goals of their department for the coming year. And once these goals are established this system will permit us to find
the most effective and the least costly
alternative to achieving American goals.

This program is designed to achieve three
major objectives: It will help us find
new ways to do jobs faster, to do jobs
better, and to do jobs less expensively.
It will insure a much sounder judgement
through more accurate information, pin-
pointing those things that we ought to do
more, spotlighting those things that we
ought to do less.

So this new system will identify our national goals with precision and will do
it on a continual basis. It will enable
us to fulfill the needs of all the American people with minimum amount of waste.

Set against the comprehensive approach to budgeting is the incremental approach. For this side, the
budget allocation process does not entail an annual review of the fundamental structure of programs (goals,
objectives, alternatives, cost/benefits), but primarily
consists of looking at the increases and decreases, the
"increments" in the budget. According to Aaron
Wildavsky, former Dean of the Graduate School of Public
Policy of the University of California/Berkeley, and
the incrementalists most vocal advocate,[5] not only is
program budgeting incapable of being performed and the
benefits not worth the costs, but it also would not be
politically acceptable. By emphasizing the specifica-

tion of goals and objectives, consensus in budgetary decisions cannot be reached and ideological debate is intensified. Further, it is contended that quantitative analysis cannot be applied to a great many alternatives in social problems. On the other hand, incrementalism, or "muddling through" the budgetary process, allows for resolution of conflicts and divergent interests in the budget process by proceeding in small steps, namely increases and decreases.

The important point to remember in all of this is that the two views do not clash over the fact that there should be more rationality in decision-making. The incrementalists do not reject, for example, policy analysis as an input to the allocation process. <u>What is the sticking point is that there should be a formalized, systematic process (such as PPBS) that should attempt to sweep "rationality" into the budget cycle.</u> In the words of Wildavsky, policy analysis should be "rescued" from PPBS.

Into this arena must now come zero base budgeting. In theory at least, ZBB is allied with the comprehensive approach and, indeed, is a major component of program budgeting. Under program budgeting, and the more formalized PPB System, there is no inherent "right" of any program for continued funding. Each program should be examined <u>in toto</u>--i.e., from a zero base--and would compete not only for a portion of the increases each year but also with every other program for its base. Theoretically, all dollars spent on one program would be in competition with all dollars spent on any other program.

The ZZB <u>concept</u> is not a new one. As far back as 1915 one observer commented on the "admonitions" given by the British Treasury to the various departments in preparing budget estimates:

> [Treasury] sends a circular letter to the officers responsible for the preparation of the estimates in each civil department. There are two stereotyped admonitions in this circular: one is general, that the state of public revenue demands the utmost economy; the other is a particular warning against assuming last year's estimates as the starting point for those of the next. The latter is a necessary warning. It must always be a temptation to one drawing up an

> estimate to save himself trouble by
> taking last year's estimate for granted,
> adding something to any item for which
> an increased expenditure is foreseen.
> Nothing could be easier, or more waste-
> ful and extravagant. It is in that way
> that an obsolete expenditure is enabled
> to make its appearance year after year in
> the estimates, long after all reason for
> it has ceased to be.[6]

Further, as we noted earlier, the theory of constructing alternative levels of budget requests (e.g., 80%,
100%, 110% of current expenditures) -- as we shall
later see, a major component of current ZBB practice --
has been put forth before.[7]

The only real, prior experiment with ZBB in the
Federal government came in 1962. In April of that
year, the U.S. Department of Agriculture, apparently
at the suggestion of the Bureau of the Budget, issued
instructions concerning the budget that was then in
preparation (i.e., the FY 64 Budget). "All programs,"
the instructions from USDA's Office of Budget and
Finance announced, "will be reviewed from the ground
up and not merely in terms of changes proposed for the
budget year....Consideration must be given for the
basic need for the work contemplated, the level at
which the work should be carried out, the benefits to
be received, and the costs to be incurred." Shortly
after the experiment in the USDA, the effort was analyzed and the results subsequently published.[8] The
authors interviewed numerous USDA budget officials and
program managers, as well as top levels in USDA
management who had been involved in the ZBB exercise.
From these interviews and their observations the
authors discovered that a zero-base budget "could be
described but could not be practiced." Only a few
specific changes were observed as a result of the
massive ZBB effort in USDA: one excess expenditure
for files was identified, and also a $100,000 reduc-
tion in an obsolete research program was brought about.
The results of the effort were aptly described: "Some
butterflies were caught, no elephants stopped." The
costs of the ZBB effort? They were heavy: 1000 ad-
ministrators spent an average of 30 hours a week for
six weeks preparing the data. Just in man-hours alone
the authors estimated that the government achieved a
return of only something more than one dollar per hour
on the effort; and this did not include of course the

opportunity costs of doing ZBB rather than something else. But the exercise was not completely futile since there was an unexpected by-product. People engaged in the ZBB experiment experienced the so-called "Hawthorne effect," whereby some "psychic" benefit was received from participation in the experiment, and a feeling of well-being was brought about by the fact that those involved felt pleased that they were following "canons of rational methods of calculation."

Practice

The current interest in ZBB is as we noted due in large measure to President Carter's heavy involvement with it when he was Governor of Georgia. And Carter's interest in it apparently stems from one man, Peter A. Pyhrr, who initiated a formalized and systematic zero-base budgeting system at Texas Instruments in the late 1960's, and was subsequently recruited by Governor Carter to implement the system for the Georgia FY 1973 budget. The ZBB process implemented very recently in public sector budgeting is very much along the lines of the gospel according to Pyhrr.[9]

Pyhrr has taken the concept of zero-base budgeting and woven around it, presumably for the first time, a formalized, systematic budget process.[10] Pyhrr claims that both the "philosophy and procedures" of his ZBB system are almost identical for industry and government, with modifications made to suit each's needs.

The heart of the ZBB process is undeniably the program manager in an organization, that untapped "reservoir" in the budget system. It is really the program manager who does the zero-base review of a program, and as such alleviates the need for a massive "staff of experts" superimposed on an organization. In the words of Pyhrr, "The [ZBB] process requires each manager to justify his entire budget request in detail and puts the burden of proof on him to justify why he should spend any money."[11] Therefore, unless the program managers do their jobs, the whole system is a house of cards.

Each program manager -- including those involved in operational as well as support services -- prepares "decision packages" for each activity or operation under the manager's responsibilities. Such a decision package sets forth goals and objectives of the activity,

-54-

alternatives examined, impact of not performing the
activity, indicators of performance, and analysis of
costs and benefits of the activity. Pyhrr claims that
it is the analysis of alternatives that provides the
innovation in the traditional budgeting technique. In
considering alternatives, the managers:

- Identify different ways of performing each
  activity; and

- Identify different levels of effort for performing the recommended way, including
  levels usually lower than, the same as, and
  higher than the current level of expenditures.

He states that such an analysis of alternatives
          ...forces every manager to consider and
          evaluate a level of spending lower than
          his current operating level; gives man-
          agement the alternative of eliminating an
          activity or choosing from several levels
          of effort; and allows tremendous trade-
          offs and shifts in expenditure levels
          among organizational units.[12]

After the decision packages have been developed,
they are ranked in descending order of importance.
Each program manager ranks the decision packages
according to his/her priorities. The decision packages
are then merged with other decision packages prepared
by other program managers within an organization unit
and a ranking is made of the aggregate. Such mergings
proceed up the organizational chain so that eventually
top management can assess the relative needs and
priorities of the different organizations.

Thus, as the decision packages are merged along
the chain and their numbers increase, so do the costs
of approving each additional decision package. In
theory at least, top management is able to determine
where in the list of packages the marginal costs begin to outstrip marginal benefits.

The benefits of ZBB for Pyhrr are that top management can assemble and view the needs and priorities
of an organization, the redundancies and overlaps
among organizational units, the minimum level needed
for each unit, and the opportunity costs of funding
one decision at the expense of another. At the same
time, a major impact in the long run is that it brings
heretofore-neglected elements into budget preparation

-- the lower and middle level managers in an organization.

In capsule form the above represents the method of the ZBB process. The following chapter outlines in detail the actual procedural steps.

[1]Robert D. Lee, Jr. and Ronald W. Johnson, Public
Budgeting Systems (Baltimore, Md.: University Park
Press, 1973), p. 13.

[2]Charles Schultze, The Politics and Economics of
Public Spending (Washington, D.C.: Brookings Institution, 1968), p. 19.

[3]Ibid., p. 41.

[4]V.O. Key, "The Lack of a Budgetary Theory,"
American Political Science Review, XXXIV (December,
1940), 1138.

[5]See his classic work, The Politics of the Budgetary Process (Boston: Little, Brown & Co., 1974)
second edition.

[6]E. Holton Young, The System of National Finance
(London: John Murray, 1936), p. 19. First published
in 1915.

[7]See especially, Verne Lewis, "Toward a Theory of
Budgeting," Public Administration Review, XII, (Winter,
1952), 42-54.

[8]Aaron Wildavsky and Arthur Hammond, "Comprehensive Versus Incremental Budgeting in the Department of
Agriculture," Administrative Science Quarterly, X
(December,1965), 321-46. Quotations that follow are
from article.

[9]See his Zero-Base Budgeting; A Practical Management Tool for Evaluating Expenses (New York: John
Wiley & Sons, 1973). This is an expanded version of
his original article -- the one which apparently
brought him to the attention of Governor Carter --
which appeared in the Harvard Business Review, November-
December 1970. Pyhrr was also one of the three staff
level authors of the original "sunset" bill, S. 2925,
introduced in the 2nd session of the 94th Congress.
See Joel Havemann, "Congress Tries to Break Ground Zero
in Evaluating Federal Programs," National Journal,
May 22, 1976, No. 21, pp. 706-13.

[10]Pyhrr acknowledges the only other formalized
effort at ZBB, the USDA experiment, but states that

"it did not resemble the methodology as described in
this book."

[11]Pyhrr, _Zero-Base Budgeting_, p. XI.

[12]_Ibid._, p. XII.

CHAPTER FOUR

THE MECHANICS OF ZBB

There are three basic steps in virtually any budget preparation, either in the private or public sector. The three steps are:

- Determining programs/functions/activities for which significant budgetary decisions are made.
  ---In ZBB we call this "Identifying <u>Decision Units</u>."

- Preparing justification statements that include information necessary for managers to make judgements on these programs/functions/activities.
  ---In ZBB we call this "Preparing <u>Decision Packages</u> Around Each Decision Unit."

- Identifying the relative priority of programs/functions/activities.
  ---In ZBB we call this "<u>Ranking</u> the Decision Packages."

It is important to realize then, at the outset, that except for performing zero-base reviews of programs in a systematic and formalized manner, and also the utilization of a new nomenclature, <u>there is nothing inherently new in ZBB</u>. Organizations have been doing "ZBB" for years.

Let us explore each step in detail and see how ZBB ties into basically all budget processes.

Identifying Decision Units

In any budget preparation there are normally
"units" around which budgetary decisions are made.
Let us look at a simple illustration. In a family's
budget there are usually certain items that bulk large
in any consideration of expenditures for that family:
for example, food, lodging, travel, education, leisure,
etc. Within each of these items however, there are
also subitems for which a family may make significant
budgetary decisions. The figure below might indicate
one family's budgetary "structure."

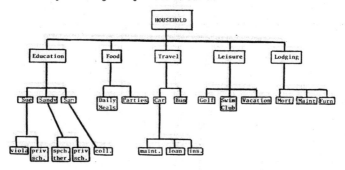

As can be seen, under the broad item of "Education"
for the family, there may be three subitems   each relating to the education of the three children of the
family, Sue, Sandy, and Sam. Perhaps for each of these
children, budgetary decisions are made by the head of
the household: for example, expenditures for Sue's
viola lessons and also her attendance at a private
school; for Sandy, her weekly speech therapy sessions
and her attendance at a private school; for Sam, his
attendance at college. Likewise, we could identify
within each of the other broad areas certain items --
"units" -- for which we make important budgetary "decisions." For example, under "Leisure" we might identify the expenditures for the twice weekly golf game,
the annual expenditure for the swim club membership,
and finally the expenditure for the family's three
week vacation during the year. If we followed out our
example, we could trace each of the "units" that make
up a family's budget.

What we could identify then in such a budget are
so-called "decision units" around which the family
makes significant budgetary decisions; in our example,

Sue's viola lessons, the father's golf games, the loan on the family car, the mortgage on the house, etc.

While the analogy may fall short in applying a family's "decision units" to a public agency's "decision units," the principle is the same. The U.S. Office of Management and Budget defines a decision unit as "the program or organizational entity for which budgets are prepared and for which a manager makes significant decisions on the amount of spending and the scope or quality of work performed." Actually, three considerations should be uppermost in the identification of an agency's decision units.

- As a first source in this identification, look at an agency's <u>organizational chart</u> together with a copy of <u>last year's budget</u>. This should give a good idea of where possible decision units might lie.

- The identification of decision units should be determined by the information needs of higher level management. In other words, if higher and top level management feel they need to go into the very "guts" of an organization and examine the budgetary decisions made there, then the decision units should be set very low in the organization. If that need is not felt -- and each agency must determine this for itself -- then the decision units should be set at the higher levels of consolidation. (In the case of the family budget, the decision units could be either the "loan" on the car, the "car" itself, or the broad item "travel.")

- The identification of an agency's decision units should be geared to the preparation not only of the agency's budget submission to OMB and the Chief Executive, but also to the eventual transmission of a budget -- even though not in a ZBB format -- to the legislature.

In any case, it cannot be emphasized too much the attention that should be addressed to the identification of decision units. This identification is fundamental to the entire ZBB process. Indeed, it might be said that <u>this identification is perhaps the most important part of ZBB since everything else that follows is built on this identification</u>. If choosing the decision units is performed in some perfunctory manner, it is most likely that ZBB will mean very little in actually putting together a budget document. However, if decision units are chosen with care, then management will know what information it will eventually be getting (and not getting) for use in preparing the actual budget document.

For the sake of illustration, let us look at the identification of decision units in a ZBB process as it might be applied to one Federal agency, the National Science Foundation.* The NSF's mission is to strengthen U.S. science through support of basic research, science education programs, and applied research on selected national problems. Its organizational structure is similar to most agencies, with Assistant Directors overseeing various programs/functions in line with this mission. (Exhibit 1 is an organizational chart of the agency.[+]) Under each of the Assistant Directors (directorates) are various divisions. After these usually come organizational entities which, for want of better terms, we might call branches, sections, and eventually specific programs. The NSF budget submission to the OMB and then to Congress is presented for the most part along these organizational lines. Thus, the budget is broken down into <u>Activities</u> (directorates), then into <u>Subactivities</u> (divisions), followed by <u>Elements</u> (branches), <u>Subelements</u> (sections), and eventually <u>Programs</u>.

For example, in the NSF, one directorate is Research Applications (budget "activity"), which administers "Research Applied to National Needs" (RANN). One of the divisions of the RANN Directorate is the Environment Division ("subactivity"), which has two subareas which we might call for the sake of illustration, branches ("elements"). One of these branches is the Disaster and Natural Hazards branch. The latter has three sections ("subelements"), one of which is Weather Modification. Under the Weather Modification subelement there are two basic programs which support research on: (1) Inadvertent Weather Modification, and (2) Advertent Weather Modification. (This budget structure is set forth in Exhibit 2.) Thus, in our

---

*It should be emphasized that the decision units, decision packages, and ranking that are used here for NSF are for illustration purposes <u>only</u>, and represent only one way ZBB might be implemented in such an agency.

[+]Exhibits begin on page 78.

illustration, two of the "decision units" for the NSF are these two programs under Weather Modification.

After we have identified the decision units for an agency -- in our illustration two of the units are, as we said, Inadvertent Weather Modification and Advertent Weather Modification -- we then prepare for each decision unit a Decision Unit Overview. The overview, usually about two pages in length, explores in general the following aspects of the decision unit:

- major goals and objectives of the decision unit and the requirements that the goals and objectives are intended to satisfy;

- feasible alternative ways to accomplish the objective(s); and

- prior progress (accomplishments) of the decision unit toward meeting the objective(s).

A sample format for the Decision Unit Overview is Exhibit 3. As can be seen, the Overview should contain the following background data on the decision unit:

(1) Identifying Information. Each Overview should contain some information (e.g., title of appropriation or fund account, or internal agency code) that identifies that particular unit from among all the other units in an agency.

(2) Long Range Goal. Goals should be directed toward general needs, are usually relatively timeless, and non-measurable.

(3) Major Objective(s). Objectives usually are of a continuing nature and may take long periods to accomplish. However, they are measurable and for the most part should be those that program managers employ .

(4) Alternatives. This may be the most difficult part of the Overview. What is required is that the program managers explore different mechanisms for performing the program/function/activity, and then show how the alternative chosen -- in most cases the current method -- contributes to satisfying the goal(s) and objective(s) of the unit.

(5) Accomplishments. Under this item should be shown the results achieved to date in ad-

dressing the objective(s). Results should employ both quantitative and qualitative measures.

For the sake of illustration we have drafted a sample Decision Unit Overview for one of the two decision units in our NSF example, the Advertent Weather Modification program. This is Exhibit 4.

Preparing Decision Packages

After we have identified decision units in an organization, and the program managers developed a Decision Unit Overview for each decision unit, the next step in the ZBB process is the preparation of a set of "Decision Packages" for each decision unit. The essence of each decision package in the set is that it addresses incremental levels of funding for the decision unit. Thus, as the Decision Unit Overview identified different ways of performing the program/function/activity, the Decision Packages identify different levels of effort of performing the program/function/activity.

The question immediately arises as to how many levels of funding, i.e., how many decision packages, should be prepared for each decision unit? There is no set answer. In general, the levels that should be prepared are:

- Minimum Level. This is the level of effort below which it is not realistic or feasible to operate the program/function/activity at all.

- Current Level. This is the level which represents a continuance of the program/function/activity at last year's funding level. (For the most part, and except perhaps for capital construction items, the level does not adjust for inflation. Thus, the Current Level is the same cost level as last year and not necessarily the same performance level.)

When appropriate, decision packages may also address:

- Intermediate Level(s). This is the level (or levels) between Minimum and Current.

-64-

- **Improvement Level(s)**. This is the level(or levels) higher than the Current Level which represents an augmented level of funding.

It is important to understand that with the exception of the Minimum Level decision package, each decision package addresses only the increment from the previous package. Thus, the "base level" package in the ZBB process is the Minimum Level package. It is here where the results of zero-funding for the program/function/activity are set forth. (In other words, if the Minimum Level is not approved, then by definition the program/function/activity would cease to exist.) On the other hand, the Intermediate Level package addresses what an increment of funding from the Minimum Level will "buy"; the Current Level package, the increment from the Intermediate Level; and the Improvement Level package, the increment above the Current Level. In a sense, then, the decision packages above the Minimum Level package represent a form of marginal utility analysis; that is, what an additional dollar spent in a program/function/activity will yield in benefits.

Exhibit 5 is a sample format for a decision package. As can be seen, a decision package -- which should also be prepared by the program manager and be no more than two pages in length -- addresses certain factors that are needed to assess the benefits (and costs) of additional levels of funding for a program/function/activity:

(1) **Identifying Information**. The decision package document should contain specific information that ties it to its respective decision unit.

(2) **Activity Description**. This section details the work that is to be performed as a result of the particular level of funding for the unit.

(3) **Resource Requirements**. Appropriate information for the program/function/activity on both obligations and outlays for the past, current, and budget years should be shown. Manpower data (i.e., program management) associated with the program/function/activity at each level should also be developed. Further, outlays for the four years beyond the budget year should also be cited. (In this last connection it is important that the

-65-

<u>future consequences</u> of the budget year ac-
tions are brought out <u>and not future actions</u>
in those years. Decision packages are not
long range planning documents and do not
obviate the need for such planning.)

(4)   <u>Short-Term Objective</u>. This section in each
      package addresses the objective that will be
      reached as a result of the particular level
      of funding. Emphasis here is, to the maxi-
      mum extent possible, on quantitative measures.

(5)   <u>Impact on Major Objective</u>. This section
      identifies how the level of funding will im-
      pact on achieving the major objective of the
      decision unit.

(6)   <u>Other Information</u>. This item can be used for
      additional material which might aid in eval-
      uating the particular level of funding ad-
      dressed. For example, included here would
      be:
      --explanation of any legislation needed in
        connection with the decision package;
      --interrelationship(s) among this decision
        package and others of another decision
        unit;
      --consequences of not approving this parti-
        cular level of funding (for the Minimum
        Level package this is crucial, since this
        is where the zero-base review of the pro-
        gram occurs).

     For the sake of illustration we have constructed
a set of four (4) decision packages for one of our
decision units in the NSF, the Advertent Weather Modification program. In our example, the Minimum Level
package (package 1 of 4) addresses what would occur if
60% ($0.9 million) of last year's (FY 78) funding were
received for this program. This is Exhibit 6. The
Current Level package (2 of 4) is our next increment
and Exhibit 7 reflects this increment; it cites what
would happen to the program if an additional $0.6
million were approved for it (i.e., 100% of last year's
funding). This increment brings the cumulative total
to last year's level, namely $1.5 million. The third
(Exhibit 8) and fourth (Exhibit 9) packages are Improvement Levels I and II, respectively, for this decision unit. Improvement Level I in our example addresses a 10% increase, and Improvement Level II
another 10% increase (or a total of 20% over the
Current Level). Thus, each of the Improvement Levels

reflects increments of $150,000.

Ranking the Decision Packages

Let us synopsize what has occurred to date in the process. First, we identified the decision units in an organization and prepared Decision Unit Overviews for the units. As a second step, we developed De-cision Packages around each decision unit; each package addressing a particular level of funding for each de-cision unit. (In our example, one of the NSF decision units was the Advertent Weather Modification program, around which we prepared Minimum, Current and two Improvement Level packages.) As can be seen from Ex-hibit 10, if we developed four decision packages around each of the decision units in a major budget activity of the NSF, the directorate dealing with "Re-search Applied to National Needs" (RANN), we would have a total of 116 decision packages for that NSF organiza-tional (and budgetary) item. This figure represents four times the number of decision units (29).

We come now to the third and final step in the ZBB process: determining the relative priorities among all the decision packages (i.e., levels of funding for pro-grams) in an organization. This determination of pri-orities we call "ranking the decision packages." The process is not unlike the one we follow when we examine our own or our family's budget. Thus, during the course of examining a family budget (our initial example), the head of the household would be determining the priority of, say, a "minimum" level of funding for the father's golf games versus, say, a "current" level for mainten-ance of the family car. Similarly, in our government agency example (and here we return to Exhibit 10), the Assistant Director of the National Science Foundation's RANN organization (consolidation level "D" in the ex-hibit) would have to determine the priorities in fund-ing for all the programs (i.e., the 29 decision units) of the organization. However, before this can occur, program managers and lower level management must first determine their priorities, i.e., rank the decision packages coming to them.

In our example, we cited two decision units, In-advertent Weather Modification and Advertent Weather Modification, for which four decision packages each were prepared. The initial step in this ranking pro-cess is for the program manager sitting atop these two

-67-

programs (decision units) to determine the priority of
funding he/she would like to pursue in addressing these
two programs. In other words, the program manager will
have to decide whether he/she would set as first priority, say, the Minimum Level of funding for the Advertent Weather Modification program before the Minimum
(and Current and Improvement) Level(s) of funding for
the Inadvertent Weather Modification program. Thus,
each program is competing against every other program
for the _total_ amount of funds that will become available, and not just a "share" of the additional funds
for all programs. This is the heart of the ZBB process.
In our example, the Advertent Weather Modification program competes not only for the additional (i.e., Improvement Level) funds that might go to it and the Inadvertent Weather Modification Program, but also for
the Minimum Level of funding that goes to the latter
program.

Suppose for the sake of illustration the person
sitting atop these two programs is a section chief in
charge of both Weather Modification programs (consolidation level "A" in Exhibit 10). The eight decision
packages come to him/her and they must be ranked. The
section chief may rank them this way:

Rank	Decision Package
1	Advertent Weather Modification (Minimum Level; 1 of 4)
2	Inadvertent Weather Modification (Minimum Level; 1 of 4)
3	Advertent Weather Modification (Current Level; 2 of 4)
4	Advertent Weather Modification (Improvement Level I; 3 of 4)
5	Inadvertent Weather Modification (Current Level; 2 of 4)
6	Inadvertent Weather Modification (Improvement Level I; 3 of 4)
7	Advertent Weather Modification (Improvement Level II; 4 of 4)
8	Inadvertent Weather Modification (Improvement Level II; 4 of 4)

What this tells us is that the section chief in
charge of these two programs chooses as his/her first

priority the Minimum Level decision package (1 of 4) of the Advertent Weather Modification program. The second priority is to fund at a Minimum Level the Inadvertent Weather Modification program. The third priority is the Advertent Weather Modification program at the Current Level. And, the fourth priority -- before the section chief would fund the Inadvertent Weather Modification program at its Current Level -- is for an Improvement Level of funding for the Advertent Weather Modification program. Thus we can see that if the section chief had to choose what to do with a given amount of funds, he/she would choose to expand the Advertent Weather Modification portion of his activity at the expense of maintaining a current level of funding in the Inadvertent Weather Modification program.

After this ranking of eight packages is completed the ranking is then passed, together with the rankings of other section chiefs of their packages, to the next level of consolidation (level "B" in Exhibit 10). Most probably this would be a branch chief, and in our illustration (Exhibit 10) the branch chief would be in charge of all programs relating to "Disasters and Natural Hazards." This person would be receiving the eight packages from the Weather Modification program, as well as packages from the other sections. In our example, the other two sections are the Earthquake Engineering Section, which has three decision units ("Design," "Siting," and "Policy"), and the Societal Response to Natural Hazards Section, which has only one decision unit. Each of these sections has of course decision packages for each of their respective decision units, so that the total amount of decision packages that the branch chief has to rank is 24 (12 from Earthquake Engineering, 8 from Weather Modification, and 4 from Societal Response to Natural Hazards).

Let us trace our four decision packages that we prepared on the Advertent Weather Modification program (Exhibits 6 through 9) and see how they fared in the branch chief's ranking. For the sake of illustration, assume the branch chief ranks the twenty-four packages for the branch in the manner set forth in Exhibit 11. The branch chief has ranked first the decision package for "Siting" (Earthquake Engineering) at the Minimum Level (1 of 4). The chief prefers as the second priority the Advertent Weather Modification decision package at the Minimum Level. The process continues until all twenty-four packages are ranked. (As we can see, the rankings for our sample decision packages for the Advertent Weather Modification program are numbers

2, 6, 12, and 18.) In addition to the rank of the decision packages, the ranking form also shows:

- resources allocated to the program during
  the previous fiscal year, which is really
  the Current Level of the program (column 3);

- total number of people allocated to the program during the previous fiscal year (column
  4);

- resources requested for the package (i.e.,
  the increment) for the budget year (column
  5);

- number of people requested for the package,
  i.e., the increment for the budget year
  (column 6);

- cumulative resources (i.e., as each package
  is ranked) requested for the budget year
  (column 7); and

- cumulative resources as a percentage of the
  previous year's budget (column 8).

The twenty-four decision packages which are ranked
are then merged with the decision packages from the
other program areas at the next consolidation level
("C"). As these packages are in turn ranked they are
passed to the next consolidation level ("D"), which
passes the packages and its ranking onto the final
level ("E"). In our example (Exhibit 10), when all
packages are merged throughout the National Science
Foundation there will be a ranking for 828 decision
packages.

We come now to a readily apparent and critical
factor in the ZBB process: How does an agency address
the volume problem -- "information saturation" --
associated with ranking a great many decision packages
of probably many dissimilar objectives and functions?
The answer is that to alleviate the work required for
management at higher levels to rank all decision packages presented to it, the ZBB process relies on a
choice between two methods: (A) consolidating the decision packages; or (B) employing "cut-off lines," so
that each review level concentrates the bulk of its
effort at ranking those packages which are considered
marginal by the lower review level. We shall address
each method in detail.

(A) Consolidation of Decision Packages

In relatively small agencies or organizations, top management may review all decision packages. However, in larger agencies and organizations "Consolidated Decision Packages" would be prepared. Consolidated decision packages are nothing more than their name implies: packages at the lower review levels are consolidated as they move to a higher level of review. The purpose of consolidation is quite obviously to avoid having higher and top management review and rank a great many individual decision packages from the organizational units far below them.

Exhibit 12 is an example of how consolidation might work. As can be seen, the 24 individual decision packages of the Disasters and Natural Hazards Branch are merged with the 8 packages from the other branch, Managing the Natural Environment, to form a ranking for the ENVIRONMENT Division. After these 32 packages are ranked at the division level, the ranking becomes the basis for the preparation of (in our example) four consolidated decision packages, ENV I, ENV II, ENV III, and ENV IV. In our exhibit we can see that there would be four consolidated packages prepared for each of the other four divisions as well. Thus, by preparing consolidated decision packages at the Division level, the next higher level of review (the Director of the entire RANN program) has to review and rank only 20 decision packages rather than 116 (as reflected in Exhibit 10).

Some important observations should be made, however, about the process of consolidating decision packages. First, as can be noted in Exhibit 12, each of the four consolidated decision packages comprising the ENVIRONMENT Division contain not only different individual programs, but also different funding levels for such programs. Thus, in ENVIRONMENT's consolidated decision package "I", there may be information on Minimum, Current and even Improvement Level individual decision packages. Therefore, while the consolidated decision packages may reflect, say, Minimum, Current, and Improvement Levels <u>for the division</u>, the dollar amounts at these funding levels will be arbitarily set. In other words, the Division consolidated decision package at the Minimum Level ("ENV I") <u>does not necessarily have to contain all the individual Minimum Level packages</u>. It may and probably will on most occasions, if for no other reason than the fact that the division will probably give first priority in its ranking to the Minimum Levels of the individual programs (i.e., "protect the base"). However, sometimes -- as seen in Exhibit 12 -- there may also be Current Levels (individual package "Y2") and Improvement Levels (individual package "Y3") of the individual packages which are found in the Minimum Level consolidated decision package for the division.

Second, format for the consolidated decision packages (as well as a consolidated decision unit overview) will most likely be similar to the format of the individual decision packages, since these consolidated packages must "track back" to the information found in the individual packages. However, most likely, these consolidated decision packages will also reflect a rationale of why individual decision packages at different levels are within certain consolidated packages. As a final word in this connection, it cannot be stressed too firmly that consolidated decision packages do not obviate the need to develop individual decision packages in subordinate units. (As we noted earlier, it is in the latter area where the real zero-base review of the program occurs.) It is only in this way that the scrutiny of all budgetary decisions can be accomplished -- if need be even by the highest levels of government.

Third, in Exhibit 12 we show only four consolidated decision packages emanating from a ranking of 32 individual decision packages. Most likely there would and should probably be more, and they would especially be finer grained (i.e., incremental packages of smaller dollar amounts) around the margin. Thus, after the Current Level consolidated decision package there should be several consolidated packages prepared around a funding level that might reasonably and realistically be expected for the budget year. For example, say the appropriation for the ENVIRONMENT Division was $10 million in FY 78. While the Division may like to have an increase of, say, 20% in FY 79 (and actually prepare consolidated decision packages reflecting such a level), it realistically expects to get no more than 5 to 10%. Therefore, consolidated decision packages might be prepared at funding levels for a Minimum budget (say, 80% of last year's appropriation), a Current Level budget (100%), Improvement Level I (say, 103%), Improvement Level II (say, 105%), Improvement Level III (say, 107%), Improvement Level IV (say, 109%), Improvement Level V (say, 111%), Improvement Level VI (say, 115%), and Improvement Level VII (say, 120%). The reason for finer grained packages at the margin (i.e., between 103% and 111% of last year's funds) is to preclude top management, who will be ranking the consolidated decision packages, having to confront and choose among Improvement Level packages of too large increments. If these finer grained packages are not prepared, top management, in their ranking of consolidated decision packages, will have a tendency to want to "split" consolidated packages (i.e., pull out certain items in these packages) to make the distribution among various consolidation levels equitably. Constructing finer grained consolidated decision packages in the range of the realistic margin can preclude this "splitting" of packages.

(B) Ranking by "Cut-Off Lines"

The second method that can be employed -- most likely by smaller agencies and organizational units -- is that each review/ranking level concentrates the bulk of its effort at ranking those packages which are considered marginal by the lower review level. In short, each review level "blocks out" a certain portion of the total number of packages coming to it and concentrates on ranking this portion. And in determining marginality, or what portion is to be "blocked out," the use of "cut-off lines" is employed. Exhibits 13 and 14 illustrate this procedure.

In Exhibit 13, an 80% cut-off line is used for each of the three sections at review level "A", one of which is our example, the Weather Modification section. What this means is that these three sections concentrate their ranking of their respective decision packages at a funding level which is 80% of last year's budget for the programs. As all the packages are merged and reviewed at the next level ("B"), which is the Disasters and Natural Hazards branch, this level employs, say, a 90% cut-off line in its ranking process. Thus, as can be seen, review level "B" will be accepting the rankings of the lower level ("A") and concentrating most of its attention on the ranking of projects between the previous 80% cut-off line and its own 90% cut-off line. In the case of Exhibit 13 for example, management at the Disasters and Natural Hazards review level prefers decision packages C2 to C3, which is preferred over B4, which is preferred over B5, and so on. In our example, the packages below the 90% cut-off line in both organizational units at review level "B", i.e., the Disasters and Natural Hazards Branch and Managing the Natural Environment Branch, will consume most of the time expended in the ranking at review level "C" (Exhibit 14). The cut-off line for that level is, say,

100%; that is, that level will be concentrating on ranking those packages which fall between 90% and 100% of last year's funding. We can see therefore that each review level will be primarily reviewing those marginal packages -- determined by cut-off lines -- passed to it by a lower level. If we wanted to follow through with Exhibit 14, the cut-off line for review level "D" might be 110%, and the Director of the NSF, who would be review level "E", would be primarily ranking those packages which would provide for an effort between 110% and 120% at last year's funding level for the Foundation.

After stating the above procedures, there are some observations that should be made. First, as is obvious, with the use of such lines zero-base budgeting very rapidly becomes incremental budgeting. But this is as it should be, since, as we mentioned in our initial comments, the zero-base review of a program really comes at the program manager's level. After that incrementalism should occur. Now this is not to say that higher review levels cannot reach down into the rankings of decision packages that have already been "approved" (i.e., through the use of cut-off lines). However, we can say that for the most part review levels concentrate much of their attention at the cut-off lines assigned them. Thus, no real ranking occurs at higher review levels of packages that are above their cut-off lines. This can be illustrated in Exhibit 13. As we said, the Disasters and Natural Hazards branch concentrates its ranking on those packages whose funding level would fall between 80% and 90% of last year's level. The branch takes as given the priorities established above the 80% cut-off line. Therefore, the branch does not really need to rank "A1" through "A5" against "B1" through "B3" against "C1". In essence, then, the branch does not have to set any priorities that fall within 80% of last year's funding level. This has both good and bad aspects. One of the major benefits of such a process is that it does not require higher levels of review to waste their time in ranking "apples against oranges" at minimum and intermediate levels -- levels that most probably will be included in the agency's budget under any circumstance. That is, for the most part these levels for the programs are "safe" in any budget the agency would prepare. The bulk of the ranking effort is placed, then, on addressing those packages on which decisions are crucial, that is, packages at the higher increments (Current Level through Improvement Levels).

The process also has a disadvantage however: it may lead lower review levels to put their "dogs" above the cut-off lines of higher review levels. By doing so, inefficient and ineffective programs can escape review by higher levels.

This leads us to our second observation: since higher review levels may not be satisfied with lower level rankings, it is important that there be decision packages prepared for each program. As the packages move up the review levels, what has already been "approved" (i.e., as determined by prior cut-off lines) can be capsulized in "Summary Analyses." Such summaries give the next review level an idea of what has already been approved without going back to the detailed rankings. ("Summary Analyses," which are of no specific format, reflect in capsulization the results of lower level rankings.) However, decision packages on each program and the ranking forms already prepared should be available if management at any level chooses to review them and reorder priorities.

Third, in our examples we have used the same cut-off line for each review level (i.e., 80% at review level "A" and 90% for review level "B"). However, there is no magic in using the same cut-off line. Management at the higher level sets the cut-off lines for the lower levels based on the review it feels programs need. Thus, management at a higher review level may set a cut-off line of, say, 70% for one program at a lower review level, and 85% for another program in the same level. Two factors that may decide the cut-off line are (1) the number of packages in each program (a larger number of packages would probably mean a much deeper, i.e., a higher percent, cut-off), and (2) whether a higher review level wishes to devote more time to establishing priorities in a particular program area. In this latter connection, assume one program has experienced difficulties in meeting objectives over the past year. Management at the higher review level might set the cut-off line higher (i.e., a lower percent) for this program for the coming year, so that the bulk of programmatic decisions reflected in the decision packages and priorities reflected in the ranking form would come under closer scrutiny by management.

As one final observation, we should perhaps comment on the ranking process itself. There is no set procedure as to who does the ranking or how it is done at higher review levels. Various techniques might be developed based on the management styles of the participants. However, in order to bring to bear as much information as possible on the ranking process -- not to mention attempting to trade further on the beneficial aspects of "participatory management" -- it would seem judicious that committees rank packages at these higher levels. Thus, to use our review levels as examples, a committee ranking at the Division level would be comprised of the Division chief (as chairperson) and the Branch heads as members; at the Directorate level, of the Assistant Director and the Division chiefs; at the agency level, of the Director and the Assistant Directors.

Also, as an initial step in constructing a ranking of all the decision packages for an agency, it might be advisable first to have each Assistant Director review all the packages of the agency (with the exception perhaps of each's Directorate) and a ranking be assembled for the Director based on the average rankings for each package. Thus, if one package is ranked #3 by one Assistant Director, #6 by another, and #9 by another, the average rank for this package in the agency-wide ranking is obviously #6. Another method might be to develop an agency-wide ranking based on a point system. Thus if there are, say, 75 packages in an agency, the number 1 ranked package would be given 75 points and the 75th ranked, one point. Average rankings can then be made for each package. In any case, and no matter what method is used, some system should be devised whereby the Director of an agency does not have to assemble his ranking from "scratch," but rather secures input from subordinates as to what agency priorities might look like from their viewpoint.

Finally, before any ranking occurs -- at any level -- criteria should be developed by and/or for the participants in the ranking. Such criteria might set forth, for example, the particular circumstances, policies, legislative mandates, etc. that should be considered in setting program balance and rationale. In some cases, the ranking will in effect be a suboptimization based on these factors affecting priorities.

In summary, then, the final step in the ZBB process is the ranking of decision packages. Ranking occurs at each review level as the packages pyramid to the agency-head level. Two methods can be employed to avoid information saturation at the top: (1) consoli-

-76-

dating decision packages, and (2) concentrating decisions at the various review levels through the use of
"cut-off lines." Ranking is usually done by a committee
so as to secure as much input as possible into the
selection process.

EXHIBIT 1

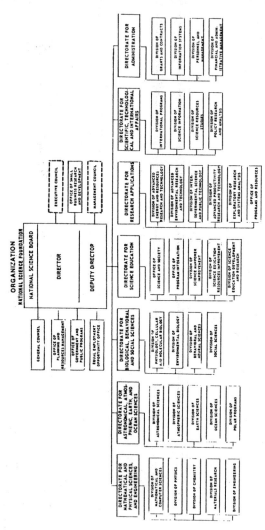

ORGANIZATION
NATIONAL SCIENCE FOUNDATION

EXHIBIT 2

POSSIBLE NSF DECISION UNIT STRUCTURE

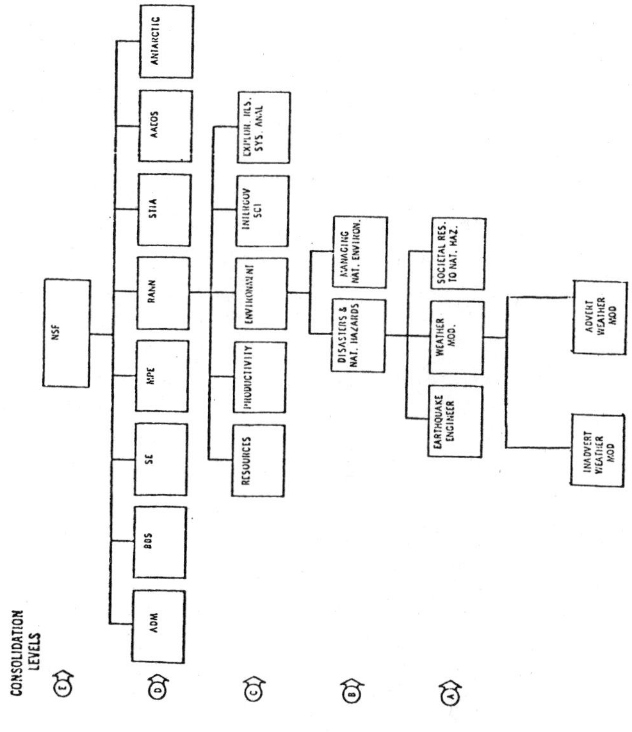

CONSOLIDATION
LEVELS

(1) NSF

(2) ADM | BOS | SE | KPE | RANN | STIA | AAEOS | ANTARCTIC

(3) RESOURCES | PRODUCTIVITY | ENVIRONMENT | INTERGOV SCI | EXPLOR RES. SYS. ANAL.

(4) DISASTERS & NAT. HAZARDS | MANAGING NAT. ENVIRON.

(5) EARTHQUAKE ENGINEER | WEATHER MOD. | SOCIETAL RES. TO NAT. HAZ.

INADVERT WEATHER MOD | ADVERT WEATHER MOD

EXHIBIT 3

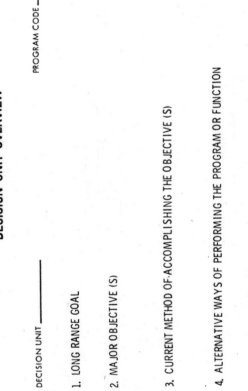

DECISION UNIT OVERVIEW

PROGRAM CODE _____

DECISION UNIT _____

1. LONG RANGE GOAL

2. MAJOR OBJECTIVE (S)

3. CURRENT METHOD OF ACCOMPLISHING THE OBJECTIVE (S)

4. ALTERNATIVE WAYS OF PERFORMING THE PROGRAM OR FUNCTION

5. ACCOMPLISHMENTS

NOTE: DECISION UNIT OVERVIEW SHOULD BE NO MORE THAN TWO PAGES LONG

PAGE ___ OF ___

EXHIBIT 4

DECISION UNIT OVERVIEW

RANN/ENVIRONMENT
DISASTERS AND NATURAL HAZARDS/WEATHER MODIFICATION
ADVERTENT WEATHER MODIFICATION

DECISION UNIT _____ PROGRAM CODE _____ 1620

Goal

To decrease the vulnerability of the nation to natural hazards and identify weather modification activities having highest potential benefit to agriculture.

Major Objective

To provide support for research so as to attempt to directly alter a possible atmospheric event, with a view toward: (a) reducing the undesirable effects of various weather hazards, particularly hail; and (b) increasing agricultural crop production by local weather modification.

Current Method

NSF has the lead responsibility for conducting the National Hail Research Experiment (NHRE), which attempts to determine the potential for suppressing hail damage by cloud seeding, and for assessing the extent to which hail suppression might be accomplished economically on an operational basis.

NSF also attempts through its Agriculture Meteorological Experiment to discover "pressure points" in the agricultural systems which are dependent on weather and climate and to determine the degree to which weather modification can increase productivity. Key issues are drought alleviation, precipitation management, and radiation control to moderate maximum and minimum temperatures in order to lengthen the growing season and reduce heat stress on crops.

Alternatives

1. Give state research laboratories the lead role for research on weather modification. Coordination among labs would be required in order to be assured all data would be evaluated and the experiments focalized. However, increased costs for coordination effort would result and lack of concerted effort might occur.

2. Allow private, commercial laboratories to carry lead. However, specialized equipment must be purchased for each location with the result that economies of scale might not occur.

-81-

EXHIBIT 4 (cont'd)

page 2: DECISION UNIT OVERVIEW (continued)

Accomplishments

During the years 1972-1976, a major hail suppression research program has been conducted in northeastern Colorado. This program, the National Hail Research cloud seeding experiment, is designed (1)to study the mechanisms of hail development, and (2)to study economic, social and legal aspects of hail suppression.

With respect to the first objective, the analyses performed on the 3 years of data from the statistical seeding experiment do not indicate a significant change in hailfall in the study area from the seeding techniques used in NHRE. On the other hand, field and laboratory experience has greatly improved our understanding of hail formation and growth, and much valuable information has been gained with respect to the economic, legal, and social issues associated with hail suppression.

The data analysis from the statistical seeding experiment was completed in FY 1977. In FY 1978, the key results of all phases of NHRE, including the statistical seeding experiment, was synthesized into a major state-of-the-art assessment concerning hail suppression. No field experiments were conducted during this period. The feasibility of drawing upon the new information gained from NHRE concerning hail formation and growth to design a practical new seeding experiment was assessed in FY 1978.

Observations of aircraft contrail formation, and the increased cloudiness produced by the introduction of aerosols and nuclei to the atmosphere, suggest that high level clouds and low lying fog can be enhanced or formed under certain conditions. Such local weather modification could markedly increase agricultural crop production by controlling radiation heat loss or gain. The potential benefits to agriculture of an ability to affect weather conditions were assessed in FY 1977. Based upon these studies, research planning studies on agricultural weather modification were initiated in FY 1978 to: develop a better understanding of weather variability and its significance to food production; and develop specific supporting weather modification technologies with an emphasis on radiation control (fog and high level clouds) on precipitation augmentation.

EXHIBIT 5

DECISION PACKAGE

PACKAGE _____ OF _____

PROGRAM CODE _____

1. ACTIVITY DESCRIPTION (PROVIDED BY LEVEL OF FUNDING):

2. RESOURCE REQUIREMENTS: ($ IN MILLIONS)

	PAST YEAR 1977	CURRENT YEAR 1978	BUDGET YEAR 1979	
			THIS PKG.	CUM. TOTAL

3. SHORT TERM OBJECTIVE THAT WILL BE ACCOMPLISHED WITH LEVEL OF FUNDING

4. IMPACT ON MAJOR OBJECTIVE THAT WILL BE ACCOMPLISHED WITH LEVEL OF FUNDING

5. OTHER INFORMATION

NOTE: DECISION PACKAGE SHOULD BE NO MORE THAN TWO PAGES LONG

PAGE _1_ OF _____

EXHIBIT 6

DECISION PACKAGE

RANN/ENVIRONMENT
DISASTERS AND NATURAL HAZARDS/WEATHER MODIFICATION
ADVERTENT WEATHER MODIFICATION

PACKAGE __1__ OF __4__ (MINIMUM LEVEL)   PROGRAM CODE __1620-1__

ACTIVITY DESCRIPTION

Complete analysis and evaluation of data from National Hail Research Experiment (NHRE), and finalize state-of-the-art assessment concerning hail suppression efforts. No further field experiments undertaken. Maintain minimal effect in local weather modification in support of agriculture. No initial field experiments undertaken.

RESOURCE REQUIREMENTS: Dollars (in millions)

	PAST YEAR 1977	CURRENT YEAR 1978	BUDGET YEAR 1979 THIS PKG.	BUDGET YEAR 1979 CUM. TOTAL
Planning grants ($)	x	x	x	x
Operating grants ($)	x	1.5	.9	.9
Total Obligations ($)	x	1.5	.9	.9
Budget Authority	x	1.5	.9	.9
Outlays	x	x	x	x
Positions (# of people)	1	1	1	1

Five-year estimates

	1979	1980	1981	1982	1983
Budget Authority	.9	.6	.8	1.0	1.3
Outlays	x	x	x	x	x

PAGE 1 OF 4

EXHIBIT 6 (cont'd)

·· page 2; Decision Package, 1 of 4 (continued)

Short-term Objective:

To ensure that the results of the NHRE are fully analyzed and evaluated, and at the same time maintain some minimal effort in the government's program of enhancing crop production through local weather modification.

Impact on Major Objective:

Some contribution would be made toward reducing the undesirable effects of hailstorms, in so far as data from the NHRE will have been analyzed and evaluated. The objective of increasing crop production by local weather modification will not be met on schedule, since field experiments cannot be started.

Other Information:

O Failure to approve this package would mean that the substantial cost involved over the last four years in obtaining data from the NHRE would be wasted, and the Federal government's responsibility to address hail hazards would be substantially affected. Since private, commercial sources are unable to carry on such extensive research, the nation would continue to suffer substantial damage each year as a result of hailstorms without any possibility of ameliorating such damage. In addition, preliminary research on agricultural weather modification would be wasted and no effort made to maintain a viable Federal presence in this area.

O Compared to the CURRENT level of effort, this package would provide for no field initial experiments in agricultural weather modification (e.g., radiation control to prevent frost or mitigate heat stress on plants).

O Failure to approve this package would affect the results of research in "inadvertent weather modification," particularly in the assessing of all results of the Metropolitan Meteorological Experiment.

EXHIBIT 7

DECISION PACKAGE

RANN/ENVIRONMENT
DISASTERS AND NATURAL HAZARDS/WEATHER MODIFICATION
ADVERTENT WEATHER MODIFICATION

PACKAGE 2 OF 4 (CURRENT LEVEL)   PROGRAM CODE 1620-2

ACTIVITY DESCRIPTION

Complete analysis and evaluation of data from IHRE, and finalize state-of-the-art assessment concerning hail suppression efforts. No further field experiments undertaken.

Continue current level of effort in local weather modification in support of agriculture with provision for initial field experiments.

RESOURCE REQUIREMENTS: Dollars (in millions)

	PAST YEAR 1977	CURRENT YEAR 1978	BUDGET YEAR 1979 THIS PKG.	BUDGET YEAR 1979 CUM. TOTAL
Planning grants	x	x	x	x
Operating grants	x	1.5	.6	1.5
Total Obligations	x	1.5	.6	1.5
Budget Authority	x	1.5	.6	1.5
Outlays	x	x	x	x
Positions (# of people)	1	1	0	1

Five-year estimates	1979	1980	1981	1982	1983
Budget Authority	1.5	1.0	1.2	1.4	1.7
Outlays	x	x	x	x	x

EXHIBIT 7 (cont'd)

page 2; Decision Package, 2 of 4 (continued)

Short-Term Objective:

To ensure that the results of the NHRE are fully analyzed and evaluated, and at the same time continue the CURRENT level of effort in the government's program of enhancing crop production through local weather modification.

Impact on Major Objective:

Some contribution would be made toward reducing the undesirable effects of hailstorms, in so far as data from the NHRE will have been analyzed and evaluated. The objective of increasing crop production by local weather modification will be on track, since initial field experiments can now be undertaken. Passage of results to mission agencies (after proof of concept stage) will occur by end of FY 83.

Other Information:

If the package is not approved the planned schedule for undertaking of field experiments will have to be revised, with the result that slippage will occur in achieving objectives.

EXHIBIT 8

DECISION PACKAGE

RANN/ENVIRONMENT
DISASTERS AND NATURAL HAZARDS/WEATHER MODIFICATION
ADVERTENT WEATHER MODIFICATION

PACKAGE __3__ OF __4__   (IMPROVEMENT LEVEL I)   PROGRAM CODE __1620-3__

ACTIVITY DESCRIPTION

Complete analysis and evaluation of data from NHRE, and finalize state-of-the-art assessment concerning hail suppression efforts. No further field experiments undertaken.

Undertake an expanded level of effort in weather modification in support of agriculture, with provision for several field experiments in radiation control (fog and high level clouds) on precipitation augmentation.

RESOURCE REQUIREMENTS: Dollars (in millions)

	PAST YEAR 1977	CURRENT YEAR 1978	THIS PKG.	BUDGET YEAR 1979 CUM. TOTAL
Planning grants	x	x	x	x
Operating grants	x	1.5	.15	1.65
Total Obligations	x	1.5	.15	1.65
Budget Authority	x	1.5	.15	1.65
Outlays	x	x	x	x
Positions (# of people)	1	1	6	1

Five-year estimates	1979	1980	1981	1982	1983
Budget Authority	1.65	1.15	1.35	1.55	.6
Outlays	x	x	x	x	x

EXHIBIT 8 (cont'd)

page 2; Decision Package, 3 of 4 (continued)

Short-term Objective:

To ensure that the results of the NHRE are fully analyzed and evaluated, and at the same time to increase the level of effort in local weather modification in support of agriculture so as to bring field experiments to proof-of-concept-stage earlier.

Impact on Major Objective:

Some contribution would be made toward reducing the undesirable effects of hailstorms, in so far as data from the NHRE will have been analyzed and evaluated. The objective of increasing crop production by local weather modification will be closer to realization; some additional field experiments will result in contracting the schedule for passage of proof-of-concept to mission agencies. Passage will occur in FY 82.

Other Information

If the package is not approved, program will still be on schedule, but acceleration of passage of results to mission agencies will not occur.

EXHIBIT 9

DECISION PACKAGE

RANN/ENVIRONMENT
DISASTERS AND NATURAL HAZARDS/WEATHER MODIFICATION
ADVERTENT WEATHER MODIFICATION

PACKAGE ___4___ OF ___4___ (IMPROVEMENT LEVEL II)   PROGRAM CODE ___1620-4___

ACTIVITY DESCRIPTION

Complete analysis and evaluation of data from NHRE, and finalize state-of-the-art assessment concerning hail suppression. No further field experiments undertaken.

Undertake a much accelerated level of effort in weather modification in support of agriculture, with provision for additional field experiment precipitation augmentation. Proof-of-concept stage reachable within 2 years.

RESOURCE REQUIREMENTS: Dollars (in millions)

	PAST YEAR 1977	CURRENT YEAR 1978	THIS PKG.	BUDGET YEAR 1979 CUM. TOTAL
Planning grants ($)	X	X	X	X
Operating grants ($)	X	1.5	.15	1.8
Total Obligations ($)	X	1.5	.15	1.8
Budget Authority	X	1.5	.15	1.8
Outlays	X	X	X	X
Positions (# of people)	1	1	1	2
Five-year estimates	1979	1980	1981	1982	1983
Budget Authority	1.8	1.30	1.45	.6	0
Outlays	X	X	X	X	X

EXHIBIT 9 (cont'd)

page 2; Decision Package, 4 of 4 (continued)

Short-term Objective:

To ensure that the results of the NHRE are fully analyzed and evaluated, and at the same time to substantially heighten the level of effort in local weather modification in support of agriculture so as to move to proof-of concept stage in 1981.

Input on Major Objective

Some contribution would be made toward reducing the undesirable effects of hailstorms, in so far as data from the NHRE will have been analyzed and evaluated. The objective of increasing crop production by local weather modification will be realized sooner, since additional field experiments will result in proof-of-concept stage being reached in FY 81. At that time, passage of results to mission agencies will occur and NSF will consolidate state-of-art assessment in 1982. No further program initiatives planned beyond that date.

Other Information:

If the package is not approved, program will still be on schedule, but realization of objective will not occur until one year later, i.e., 1983.

EXHIBIT 10

FLOW OF DECISION PACKAGES TO AGENCY HEAD

CONSOLIDATION (AND REVIEW)
LEVEL

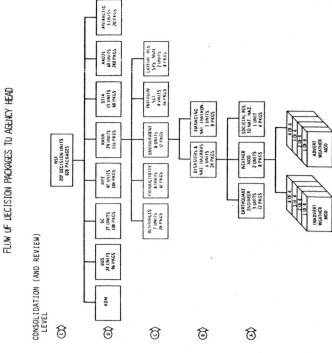

FY 1979 RANKING SHEET
MILLIONS

EXHIBIT 11

(1) RANK	(2) DECISION PACKAGE	FY 78 RESOURCES		FY 79 BUDGET REQUEST		CUMULATIVE TOTAL	
		$ (3)	POSITIONS (4)	$ (5)	POSITIONS (6)	$ (7)	% OF CURRENT (8)
1	A1 SITING (EE) (1 OF 4)	6.0M	4	3.6M	3	3.6M	15
2	B1 ADV WM (1 OF 4)	1.5	1	0.9	1	4.5	19%
3	C1 SOC. RESP (1 OF 4)	1.5	1	0.9	1	5.4	23%
4	A2 DESIGN (EE) (1 OF 4)	9.0	7	5.4	5	10.8	45
5	A3 POLICY (EE) (1 OF 4)	5.0	4	3.0	3	13.8	58%
6	B2 ADV WM (2 OF 4)			0.6	0	14.4	60
7	C2 SOC. RESP (2 OF 4)			0.6	0	15.0	63
8	C3 SOC.RESP (3 OF 4)			0.15	0	15.15	63%
9	B3 INADV. WM (1 OF 4)	1.0	1	0.6	1	15.75	66%
10	A4 SITING (EE) (2 OF 4)			2.4	1	18.15	76%
11	A5 SITING (EE) (3 OF 4)			0.6	0	18.75	78
12	B4 ADV WM (3 OF 4)			0.15	0	18.9	79
13	B5 INADV. WM (2 OF 4)			0.4	0	19.3	80%
14	C4 SOC. RESP (4 OF 4)			0.15	1	19.45	81%
15	A6 POLICY (EE) (2 OF 4)			2.0	1	21.45	89%
16	A7 DESIGN (EE) (2 OF 4)			3.6	2	25.05	104%
17	B6 INADV. WM (3 OF 4)			0.1	1	25.15	105%
18	B7 ADV. WM (4 OF 4)			0.15	1	25.3	105%
19	A8 SITING (EE) (4 OF 4)			0.6	0	25.9	108%
20	B8 INADV. WM (4 OF 4)			0.1	0	26.0	108%
21	A9 POLICY (EE) (3 OF 4)			0.5	0	26.5	110%
22	A10 DESIGN (EE) (3 OF 4)			0.9	0	27.4	114%
23	A11 POLICY (EE) (4 OF 4)			0.5	0	27.9	116%
24	A12 DESIGN (EE) (4 OF 4)			0.9	1	28.8	120%
	TOTALS	$24.0M	18	$28.8M	24		

EXHIBIT 12

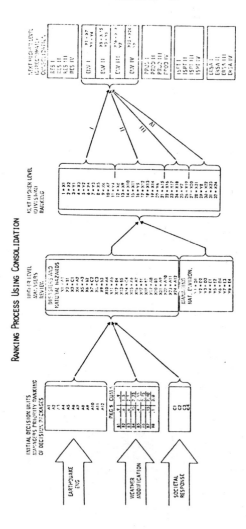

EXHIBIT 13

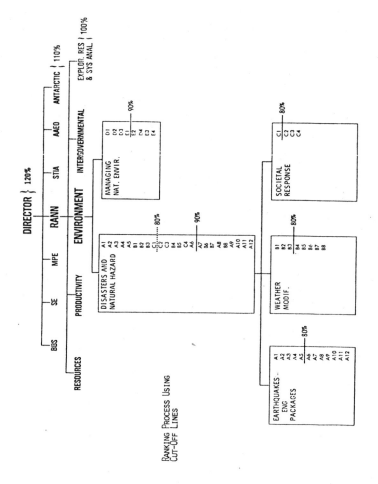

EXHIBIT 14

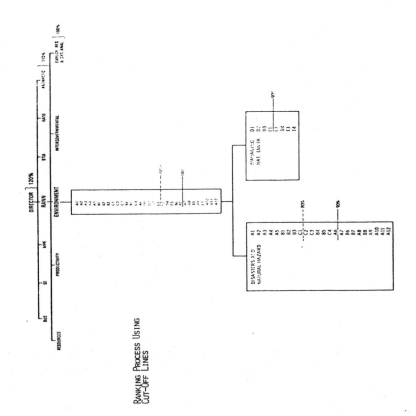

RANKING PROCESS USING
CUT-OFF LINES

CHAPTER FIVE

THE BENEFITS AND COSTS OF ZBB

BENEFITS

Like budget innovations before it, ZBB claims to aid in addressing resource allocation problems. In the words of Pyhrr, it "provides management with a flexible operating tool to answer the questions: Where and how can we most effectively spend our money? [and] How much should we spend?"[1] There are other benefits, to be sure -- and these will be addressed later -- but the resource allocation question is fundamental in any evaluation of the benefits of ZBB. It must be examined first. In short, we must ask: Will we make "more rational" decisions by using ZBB? And, will ZBB aid us in _effectively_ and/or _efficiently_ spending our money?

Increases Management Information

In answering the questions it is perhaps useful to view ZBB in the context of previous innovations. First, it is important to remember that, as one observer has commented, "the recent history of efforts to improve techniques for strengthening management in the public sector is characterized by [among other things] an implicit assumption that the appearance of neatness can create the fact of rationality."[2] And of this there can be no doubt: ZBB is a very "neat," tidy system. Zero-base budgeting, at least as practiced currently, is systematic and formalized. It has a structured

nature that characterized its immediate predecessors,
MBO and PPBS. However, "program memorandum," "mile-
stone charts," and "decision packages," do not necessarily make for more "rational" budgeting. The process
itself may be very rational in that it carefully displays a good deal of data that might be used for decisions. The problem comes, however, in superimposing
a rigid, structured system (which captures such data)
on government agencies and making it mean something to
budgeting. For all systems have a proclivity to de-
generate into processes alone and soon the connection
with budgeting -- where the real allocation of resources
occurs -- is lost. Ultimately budgeting continues in
its same mode with little if any impact from the process. This is of course what happened to PPBS; in the
words of Allen Schick in his already-classic article,
"PPB failed because it did not penetrate the vital
routines of putting together and justifying a budget."[3]
It appears that the more recent innovation, MBO, has
suffered a similar fate. While originally conceived
of as a short term, tactical management tool, MBO, as
eventually implemented by OMB Director Ash in 1973,
soon took on certain dimensions of an allocation strategy.[4] Under Ash, "budget decisions would ideally flow
from a continuous process of program analysis tuned to
established objectives and achieved results."[5] A staff
of "management associates" was recruited "to ensure
that agencies observed the process."[6] MBO was soon
wedded to the budget process and agency objectives were
submitted to OMB together with estimated budget outlays.
Perhaps this fact -- that MBO was asked to do more than
it was capable of doing -- led to its current limbo-like
state in the Federal establishment. In any case, MBO's
life has been even shorter than PPB's. Though its
demise is still not officially recognized, there is
enough evidence to indicate that it fared little better
than PPB with the budgeteers.

It is essential then for any evaluation of ZBB
that we not confuse rationality of the process with
rationality in the allocation of resources, or efficiency with effectiveness. If ZBB is to provide any
meaning to budgeting in the public sector, it must
first adapt itself to the political nature of budgeting. As such, then, ZBB cannot set policy, or allocate resources effectively, i.e., where and how to
spend money. That is the job solely of the political
system. ZBB should not aim at saying which program is
"better" or "more rational" in the context of societal
needs. ZBB should not be heralded -- as PPB was in 1965

when introduced government-wide by President Johnson -- as a "system [which] will identify our national goals with precision." But ZBB can provide decision-makers with information upon which to gauge policy. It can do this by displaying to decision-makers perhaps the most important piece of information they can have in addressing allocation of resources: <u>the "opportunity costs" of funding one program at the expense of another</u>. And this is an important, critical contribution towards budget formulation. For through its ranking system, ZBB presents to decision-makers -- at all levels and with myriad interests -- the opportunities foregone by funding one program (or level of a program) versus another. The ranking process in ZBB allows the decision-maker to see what is given up (the opportunities foregone) by choosing a particular level for funding. In a word, the "tradeoffs" are displayed. Thus, for example, the decision-maker is not required to address whether the objectives of funding research on earthquake prediction are "better" than the objectives arising from expanded research on weather modification, or that one program contributes "more" than another in maximizing public utility. In this sense, ZBB is not the PPB System revisited. The ranking process in ZBB allows the decision-maker to prioritize through whatever means available -- policy analysis, cost/effectiveness analysis, program evaluations, prior program success in goal achievement, or even intuition. In our example, if the decision-maker decides in favor of more earthquake prediction research, the real cost of the project (assuming a constrained budget) is less research on weather modification. And only the political process can answer whether the "benefits outweigh the costs" in this decision. Thus, unlike PPB, ZBB does not impinge on the political nature of decison-making.

If ZBB cannot directly answer the effectiveness question -- that is, what we should spend money on, or those "big choices" which David Novick claimed program budgeting aimed at[7] -- it can provide information on how we can spend it efficiently, once it has been decided by the political system to spend it. In this connection, ZBB bears a close resemblance to performance budgeting. Budgeting is a science of decisions made at the margin: what an additional dollar invested in a program will buy in benefits compared to its costs. After policy has been established, ZBB can provide agencies with efficiency-type information by displaying alternative levels of funding as found in the sets of decision packages. Thus, to go back to our example, agency management should be in a better position to allocate resources efficiently in earthquake prediction and weather modification research if they know what incremental or alternative levels of funding will purchase in each case. For example, perhaps 115% of last year's funding level (an alternative level around which a decision package might be constructed) will provide little in the way of immediate benefits in achieving this year's objectives in earthquake prediction research. However, in weather modification research, realization of that program's objective may be close at hand and 115% will achieve it. The agency is thus presented with information of an efficiency nature upon which it can make programmatic decisions and construct a budget. Needless to say, some agencies have been using methods of marginal utility analysis for years. What ZBB does though is that it would make the practice routine.

Right away, then, the above should tell us a good deal what ZBB is and is not about in so far as the question of ZBB's contribution to the allocation of resources is concerned. ZBB is not the same for both industry and government. ZBB results in the public sector are quite different from those achieved in the private sector. In the latter the objective is for the most part profits. In pursuit of this objective, ZBB reviews can result in projects/services being abolished, people let go, and efforts undertaken with relative ease. The proponents of ZBB in the public sector should not be so sanguine. The objectives of public programs are not so easily determined nor "production functions" (that determine input/output relationships for these programs) and effectiveness measures for such programs easy to come by. Further, as we know public programs have clientele groups (not to mention the agencies themselves) which follow the funding of their programs diligently and cultivate appropriate Congressional support. Only in the most unusual of circumstances will any group allow a zero-base review of its program to result in the abolishment of a program.

Rather, ZBB's major contribution in the public sector -- and it is a substantial one -- is in displaying for decision makers the tradeoffs existing among programs and the incremental decisions relating to such programs. Thus ZBB can play an important role in putting together a budget. In this connection, a major strength is that it gives to an agency a ready and facile tool in constructing alternate budgets. It allows decision makers to play, what Pyhrr calls, "what if" situations. This is significant because in recent years OMB and the Congress have constantly come to ask of agencies the effects of alternative agency funding levels. Through the use of ranking and the display of what different funding levels will "buy," ZBB can provide this information readily without having budgeteers working into the night trying to piece together budgets under different scenarios. Accordingly, so-called "Opportunity" (improvement) and "Fallback" levels of an agency's budget should be a lot easier to construct. If for no other reason than a good night's rest, then, budgeteers should welcome ZBB!

Yet, after we have said all we can say about what ZBB is likely to contribute in the way of significant management information, we are still left with the question: Does ZBB really matter? Information is fine, but does it make a difference in decision-making? Or at least does it make a difference so that the benefits outweigh the costs of collecting the information?

It would appear that the question could be answered differently depending on what we expect any budget system to provide in both the short and long term. In the short term, experience with ZBB, while admittedly limited to date, would seem to indicate that ZBB in the public sector really doesn't pay for itself. The returns for example on the "zero-base budgeting" effort in the USDA were slim. Not only are there significant direct costs in a ZBB effort -- Wildavsky noted that the USDA zero-base budgeting effort almost created a surplus storage problem as a result of the information saturation! -- but the opportunity costs are substantial: program managers, budgeteers and higher management all could be doing something else rather than ZBB. And based on what evidence is available to date on the most recent ZBB experiments, the shift in the allocation of resources as a result of using ZBB is problematical. Allen Schick, an authority on the government budget process, noted this in recent testimony on ZBB before the House Committee on the Budget.[8] George Minmier, who undertook an analysis of the ZBB effort in Georgia after it had been implemented there for three years, has also observed this fact.[9] Minmier notes that responses elicited from departmental budget analysts who had been present during implementation of ZBB in Georgia confirm this.[10] Additional evidence comes from personal interviews conducted of thirteen

department heads in Georgia who could not point to any
apparent reallocation of resources in their departments
as a result of implementing ZBB.[11] However, notwithstanding this fact, over 78% of the department budget
analysts recommended the continued use of zero-base
budgeting in some form,[12] and not one budget analyst of
the Georgia central budget office, the Office of Planning and Budget, recommended discontinuing the ZBB
effort![13] Perhaps the Georgia experience was the USDA
"Hawthorne effect" revisited: ZBB didn't make any
difference but budgeteers, program managers, and higher
management "felt better" after doing it. But ZBB has
to do more than this -- or does it?

Actually, the benefits of ZBB occur in the long
term and they occur in improvements to the budget process itself. Recently, Pyhrr himself, in presenting
perhaps a more cautious assessment of ZBB in the public
sector than was in evidence in his book, sees this as a
major benefit of ZBB.[14] Ever mindful of Keynes' ad-
monition about the interrelationship between the state
of our health and problems solved in the long run, we
too reach this conclusion. Budgeting is power brokerage
-- within an agency, among agencies and particularly
of course in Congress. All ZBB is designed to do is
force us along the line whereby the brokerage occurs in
light of the best available information. Further, with
public accountability becoming more an issue daily, the
emphasis on information in public decision making is
heightened. Needless to say, the Executive branch of
the Federal government has had a long history of this
reaching back not only through MBO and PPBS, but also
to the performance budgeting of the 1930's. Indeed,
it might even be argued that the origins can be laid to
President Taft's Commission on Economy and Efficiency,
which as we noted, drafted the first Executive budget
on the Federal level since Alexander Hamilton and which
proposed in reality the Federal government's first
effort at program budgeting.

The Congress on the other hand has only recently
come to address this situation as a critical problem.
However, they are away fast now and sprinting. What
that body has been attempting to do, as evidence by
such recent, obvious efforts as passage of the Budget
and Impoundment Control Act of 1974, establishment of
the Office of Technology Assessment, and creation of
expanded roles for the GAO and the Congressional Research Service, is, as one observer of congressional
power noted over a decade ago, "to define limits to the

non-use of information -- i.e., how irrational the system can or should be in its allocation decisions."[15]

This brings us to the point, which we will comment on further in the next chapter, concerning the acceptance by the Congress of the "results" of the ZBB effort in the Executive branch. For if ZBB is to succeed in the Executive branch of the Federal government as a tool in budget formulation, and the increased management information generated be made worthwhile, a "necessary" condition is that the ZBB effort be given something more than tacit recognition by the Congress. PPBS and MBO died or are dying of many wounds; but one main reason for the systems' inability to crack budgeting was the failure of Congress to give much more than a passing nod to both these systems as tools in constructing a budget.

Recent evidence concerning this inability and the ZBB effort in State governments bears out this ominous fact, and also what happens when the legislature is receptive to ZBB and the executive isn't. Minmier, for example, in his analysis of the ZBB effort in Georgia states that the lack of acceptance of the ZBB system on the part of that state's legislature had created a "multitude of problems in forming the final budget for the state."[16] One particular problem cited was that "department heads who are not satisfied with their allotment of funds in the executive budget [as a result of the ZBB process] know that they have another opportunity to procure additional funds during the budgetary session of the State legislature."[17] The tendency that develops as a result of this situation can easily be predicted: departmental budget analysts circumvent the Executive budget process and concentrate on the legislature. Needless to say, the benefits of ZBB as a tool in budget preparation in the Executive branch break down. In the New Mexico ZBB effort (since discontinued), difficulties occurred when the two branches were not in accord on the ZBB effort.[18] In that state, it was the Legislature which provided the fillip for instituting the ZBB effort. Beginning in 1970, and running into the next several years, the Legislature (through its Legislative Finance Committee) requested Executive agencies to justify their programs and budget requests under a zero-base system. Apparently, however, the Executive branch was opposed to the effort. It took a while, but the obvious difficulties of one branch going in one direction and another branch not following eventually emerged. Peter Pyhrr's comments, made while testifying on ZBB before the House Committee on the Budget, aptly describes the situation:

> What happened in New Mexico is a classic example of what can happen when the executive agencies or the executive offices are pulling in one direction and the legislature in another. ...In New Mexico you had a strong legislative budget staff who wanted to implement zero-base budget[ing] and an executive staff that did not want to. Therefore the agencies were given two completely different sets of budget instructions and they had to prepare the two budgets. I pity the agency managers who had to do that."[19]

Actually, however, the time may be propitious for Congressional acceptance of an Executive budget prepared and submitted under the aegis of the ZBB process. And if acceptance is achieved, some credit for this has to be given to Executive budget innovations of the past. Harry Havens, Director of the Office of Program Analysis for the GAO, notes that innovations such as PPBS and MBO have had a "residual impact [on Congress] on the future" and the role of analysis in general in evaluating public expenditures.[20] Thus there is currently what we might call an "analytical overhang" that has permeated Congress as a result of, among other things, past Executive budget systems. The most promising aspect of ZBB in the Executive branch, then, is that Congress, unlike on previous occasions, may be in a more receptive mood to accept budgets prepared under such a system. (This does not mean, though, in a ZBB format.) Therefore, Congressional support, while not providing a "sufficient" condition for ZBB's penetrating the vital routines of budget formulation in the Executive branch, may certainly provide a "necessary" one.

In summary, then, we view as the first and major benefit of ZBB the improvement of management information upon which decision-makers can set policy. In this connection, the ZBB process provides a particular facet of management information which, in light of the political nature of public budgeting, must be considered crucial in decision-making: the displaying of the opportunity costs of funding one program over another. If for no other reason that that, ZBB is innovative. Of only slightly lesser benefit is the advantage accruing to budgeting as a result of displaying the marginal utility (or disutility) of programs addressed at alternate funding levels. This is of course an efficiency

benefit, but it is still welcome to budgeteers. For in
recent years Congress has come to ask "what if" questions of agencies. Through its ranking process, ZBB
should give budgeteers a welcome and, more importantly,
a facile and timely tool in providing answers to such
questions. If ZBB can do so then we must certainly
conclude that the budget process is improved.

Enhances Participation and Control in Budgetary Processes

In addition to its aiding in the display of information keyed to questions of resource allocation, ZBB
trades on another strength -- its use as a management tool.
And in examining the arguments in this area we come
away with the impression that ZBB, as a mangement tool,
attempts to cull the best from PPBS and MBO, as those
systems were originally conceived of as being part of
the management process. In theory at least the arguments are strong.

First, let's look at ZBB and MBO as management
instruments. The major strength of MBO, at least as
originally conceived, is that it relies on "participatory management," i.e., superiors and subordinates
jointly define objectives, identify each's area of
responsibility as regards the results expected from
certain efforts in pursuit of the objectives, and explicitly state how achievement of such objectives will
be measured. The benefits of this approach are that
    ...through the participative process,
    management hopes to increase organiza-
    tional effectiveness by developing
    meaningful individual and organizational
    goals, clarifying responsibilities, pro-
    moting supervisor-subordinate collabora-
    tion and improving the administrative feed-
    back process.[21]

Peter Drucker, perhaps MBO's most well-known ideologue,
would add another, more important dimension to MBO:
the system's ability to produce responsibility and
commitment within an organization, i.e., "willingness
of the individual within the organization to focus his
or her own vision and efforts towards the attainment
of the organizations's goals."[22]

ZBB aims at effecting similar results. Pyhrr,
in his analysis of the management role for ZBB,

-105-

explicitly notes the enhanced motivation brought about on the part of management and subordinates when all participate in setting objectives.[23] (Needless to say, after objectives are set, management systems, such as MBO, can be implemented to measure performance against objectives.)

This advantage of ZBB has been observed by others as well. Minmier, in his analysis of the Georgia ZBB effort, cites the "increase in the involvement of personnel at the activity level [i.e., in the program offices] in the State's budgeting process" as one of ZBB's benefits in that state.[24] In evaluating the New Mexico experiment, LaFaver lists this "involvement" as one of ZBB's "significant strengths."[25] Also, in an analysis of a recent ZBB effort in local government, the inauguration of ZBB as a tool in the preparation of the Wilmington, Delaware city budget in 1975, this same factor was brought out. In commenting further on this interrelationship between ZBB and MBO, the analysts noted that ZBB is an "excellent basis for an MBO program," since the information presented in decision packages should aid in measuring "performance against objectives...much more quantitatively."[26]

We agree. Notwithstanding Drucker's comments that "it is not necessarily true, as so many romantics in management seem to believe, that the subordinate always knows better,"[27] we view ZBB's fostering of an MBO-like **"bottom-up"** approach to management and budgeting as a significicant plus. (In fairness to all irate subordinates, we should also note that Drucker didn't feel that the boss always knows what's better either!) ZBB can complement an MBO approach to management: not only does the program manager share responsibility for goal achievement, but, under ZBB, the managers also share programmatic priority setting. From the standpoint of public accountability for government managers, then, ZBB has much to say for itself.

Further, at the same time that a "bottom-up" approach is being fostered, ZBB also has aspects of a "top-down" approach -- something that program budgeting (PPBS) traded on in its claim for improving management. While program budgeting does of course entail cooperation among all personnel for implementation and operation, there is, undeniably, a centralizing tendency in program budgeting. For after all this is what program budgeting is about: by identifying and evaluating the inputs that "crosswalk" into an agency's outputs and objectives, top management gains fuller control of subordinate units and can direct their efforts. Charles Schultze, current Chairman of the Council of Economic Advisers, noted this as a major strength of PPBS when he was Director of the Bureau of the Budget under President Johnson. Schultze felt program planning and control of evaluation staffs under a PPB System "strengthened the role of the agency head in relations with the operating units." He added that PPBS had in some cases "helped modestly to redress the balance" that he felt existed prior to the implementation of PPBS, i.e., "the balance of power lie[ing] too much against most agency heads" in their dealing with such units.[28] ZBB contains similar, centralizing tendencies and has a PPBS-like quality in its top-down approach to management;"[T]op down because top management must determine the goals and objectives of each major organizational entity and establish the general operating guidelines and expenditure levels acceptable in achieving the objectives."[29]

As an aside, some brief words should also be said concerning how ZBB claims to be different from PPBS and MBO in management style. For ZBB proponents, the staff requirements for ZBB are not overloaded at the top; the bulk of the work is done "down in the pits" (which should prove to be a mixed blessing for some bureaucrats). ZBB shies away from the "very special staff of experts" that President Johnson envisioned for PPBS and who would aid us in goal definition, or the "management associates" recruited by Roy Ash and Fred Malek in carrying out MBO government-wide. In critiquing the ZBB effort in Georgia, Pyhrr notes with evidence satisfaction that budget bureaus outside Georgia marvelled at the small number of personnel needed to administer the ZBB process.[30] For Pyhrr, a "large centralized administrative staff defeats ... [the] intent" of ZBB, since it is the program managers upon which the system relies.[31] We might only add, acidly, in this connection that the Federal budget is a bit larger than the state of Georgia's, and if ZBB is to succeed some slight modification may have to be made in either the output per man hour of the OMB staff monitoring the ZBB effort or the number of departmental budget analysts coordinating the effort. We base our comment on the often-misplaced fact about the Georgia experiment: it was undertaken with 65 agencies and a budget of only $1 billion in state funds and approaching $2 billion in total funds.[32] (But, then again, maybe we'll just round to a higher figure at the Federal level!)

The only comment we have on this claimed strength of ZBB -- i.e., that it is a "top down, bottom up" approach to budgeting -- is that it also contains within itself the seeds of its own destruction. For ZBB to provide meaning to budget preparation, the process must be viewed by subordinate units as something more than a repetitive, routine, mechanistic process designed by top management to consume their time. And to avoid this pitfall, top management must be certain to ensure that there is an adequate feedback process between superiors and subordinates, i.e., that subordinates have an input not only in setting priorities, strategies, and performance measures, but also that they be adequately informed and a rationale given when top management's choices differ. And, equally important, the implementation of ZBB in the Federal establishment must be considered in light of the peculiarities and differences found among agencies in that establishment. In this connection, management must seek input from subordinate units on how to initiate and carry out the process.

For if anything can kill ZBB, failure to consider these factors can; ZBB will fall from similar wounds like those inflicted upon PPBS and MBO. In Schick's autopsy of PPBS he found massive damage had been done by the fact that "civilian department heads were ordered to graft an alien, standardized system onto their regular budgetary processes."[33] Cutting further, he isolated a contributing cause of the system's shutdown: "PPB died because of the manner in which it was introduced, across-the-board and without much preparation."[34] Watchers of the terminally-ill MBO come up with a similar factor in assessing the downhill slide of that patient: "MBO and related managerial controls were inaugurated without necessary understanding of motivation, authority, and power in public organizations."[35] Complicating the illness is the fact that "though proclaimed a participative process, government-wide MBO should be more properly identified as a strategy for hierarchical control."[36] They are not sparing in their comments as to how this situation was brought about:

> The attitude of the Nixon top management was one of low trust and contempt toward civil servants. Control and domination of the system became particularly central concerns in his second term.[37]

Criticism of the ZBB efforts to date point out the

-108-

necessity for the feedback process in all aspects of the system. In private sector ZBB, the tailoring of ZBB to particular organizational needs and assuring adequate feedback has been observed.[38] In the Georgia experience, Pyhrr implies as much in his critique of the problems of the first year's effort of ZBB in that state.[39] Minmier, in his analysis of the first three Georgia budgets conducted under ZBB, documents the case more definitively. He reaffirms the fact that the problems of implementing ZBB in the public sector are not the same as those confronting it in the private sector. He notes that ZBB was thrust upon state agencies with little preparation or input by them. The implementation phase failed to consider the experience not to mention power positions that had been built up by agency personnel in their budgetary relationships with the Legislature. This immediately created dissatisfaction among subordinate units and Minmier notes that "many of the problems experienced during the first year of zero-base budgeting could have been averted" had this dissatisfaction not occurred.[40] A major recommendation of his study is that for future ZBB efforts, participation of budget personnel be sought during the planning and implementation phase of ZBB. Minmier is also critical of the lack of feedback provided lower organizational levels concerning the reordering of priority rankings by top management levels. He sees this as a particular failure and one that is especially deleterious to acceptance of ZBB at these lower levels.[41]

The criticisms on this aspect of ZBB and the need for feedback appear justified. If ZBB is to trade on the fact that, as Pyhrr says, it "taps a large reservoir of program knowledge and analytic resources...the operating managers throughout the agency hierarchy,"[42] then it had best secure input on the problems and prospects of ZBB implementation from these managers. At the same time, feedback should be adequately ensured so as to preempt dissatisfaction with the system early. If ZBB is to mean anything to budgeting and become a viable system, it would be judicious to avoid the faults of PPB and MBO in this connection.

In summary, then, we view the "participatory management" emphasis as well as the centralizing tendency of ZBB to be another significant strength of the process. We would only caution, however, that the management aspects of implementing and operating ZBB be clearly conceived, lest the system impale itself early on its own eagerness for change.

Heightens the Roles of Planning and Analysis in Budgeting

The third and final major strength of ZBB is that the process should heighten the particular roles of planning and analysis in budgeting. And this is especially important now when the question of "openness" in government decision making is so topical. Let us explore this point.

We have already mentioned that ZBB cannot address the "big choices" -- to use Novick's term again -- in questions of allocation of resources; it lacks any "goal identification/definition" aspects that characterized the claims of an innovation such as PPB. However, in fairness to ZBB proponents, and except for some heady language about answering questions concerning "where and how we can most effectively spend our money" -- which we can attribute to the initial exuberance characteristic of any new system -- it should be said that ZBB does not really purport to address goal identification/definition. In the first few pages of his book, Pyhrr notes that ZBB must be supplemented by an adequate planning process.[43] For him, planning "identifies output desired," i.e., sets goals, makes policy decisions, and establishes programs. Budgeting, on the other hand, "identifies the input required," i.e., analyzes programs to determine how they might achieve the goals of an organization, examines alternatives within programs, and displays tradeoffs among programs. It is obvious, therefore, that if ZBB is to succeed as a budget formulation process, specific guidelines on goals and objectives are necessary. Thus, ZBB does something more than encourage planning and policy analysis: it mandates an adequate planning system that contributes to setting goals and exploring possible funding requests for agencies.

For it must be understood that ZBB is basically a short-range tool -- i.e., one budget at a time -- that addresses efficiency rather than effectiveness questions. As we have noted, ZBB is like performance budgeting in this regard, i.e., budgeting by function and activity with emphasis on work performance measures. It can tell us how well we are doing the job, but not whether the job is really needed. ZBB concentrates on constructing a budget through its display of "outputs" rather than "impacts." An output is a result in terms of what will be produced with resources, e.g., amount of services provided with a certain dollar level. Impact, on the

other hand, addresses results in terms of the effect
that resources and outputs have on a problem or need.
(We would disagree with Pyhrr therefore on the definition of "outputs.") The heavy reliance on quantitative
data in the decision packages reflects this efficiency
orientation. Thus, like performance budgeting, ZBB
emphasizes the management function of budgeting that
Allen Schick, in his analysis of the stages of budget
reform, documented so well.[44]

In a related connection, the only recognition given
by ZBB of out-year budget choices is the notation in
decision packages of funds projected for these years
as a result of current (not future) decisions. There
is no mention in decision packages of future choices
that affect programmatic directions and allocation requests. Thus, long range planning is absent in ZBB.
Further, ZBB does not provide directly for evaluations
of past efforts. ZBB must draw upon other elements in
the decision-making process for assistance in these
areas. Pyhrr brings this out strongly in his comments
concerning the "macro" nature of planning and the
"micro" aspect of ZBB.[45]

In addition to enhancing as well as mandating
planning and policy analysis at the goal identifica-
tion/definition level, ZBB also heightens the role of
analysis in general at the program manager's level
and at the consolidation levels. We say this because
ZBB is a very "open" system, i.e., program managers'
decisions and priorities, as well as those found at
each consolidation level, can be closely scrutinized
if need be. We would expect that under a ZBB process
of putting together a budget, managers as well as management would be called upon more and more to justify
their rankings of priorities. (Indeed, as evidenced
by the ZBB efforts in New Mexico and New Jersey, this
"openness" is a major reason for some agencies resistance to the ZBB system.[46]) Now this is not to argue
that, say, a cost/benefit analysis has to be applied
to each program and every alternative within a program
that is looked at by managers and management. Needless to say, intuition (or other factors) may be as
crucial in priority setting as any form of quantitative
analysis. However, at the same time there is only so
much "non-analysis" priority setting that the public
decision-making system will allow. Sooner or later
management, if for no other reason than to cover that
part of their anatomy which always seems to be open to
attack, will demand analysis as back-up for priority

rankings. Thus, ZBB puts a strong burden of proof
upon program managers for their decisions. While some
program managers may feel that they may never be que-
ried concerning their decisions, it also seems that to
prepare for that contingency such managers may come to
think more and more about the accomplishments of their
programs and the measurement of benefits and costs of
such programs.

We can of course cite very little evidence for
this conclusion. While it does not seem unreasonable
that this situation will occur, still, since ZBB in
the public sector is still in its nascent stages, there
is relatively little material to draw on. The case of
the New Mexico ZBB experiment does give some evidence,
though. In that state some agencies made only a token
effort toward zero-base budget presentations. The result was that "[w]hen agencies often failed to address
the critical issues of their programs," top management
(in this case the state's Legislative Finance Committee)
"attempted to define and research the issues."[47] We
would expect a similar situation to occur at the Federal level. Congress, in its effort to make government
"more responsive," is attempting more and more to
examine Executive decisions in the budget <u>preparation</u>
stages.[48] If such decisions are to be reviewed, then
it would appear that agencies would be especially careful of the basis for their decisions.

In summary, then, we see as another strength of
ZBB its ability to heighten the role of planning and
policy analysis in addressing broad priorities, and to
increase the need for analysis in general in programmatic decisions. Of course this is a normative conclusion on our part; we view planning and analysis as
playing major roles in budgeting and enhancing the
budgetary process. However, the cry for "public accountability," together with the emphasis on "openness"
in government decision-making (such as through "sun-
shine" legislation), indicates that the implications
of the conclusion may be justified even though one may
not agree with it.

COSTS

The above represent the major strengths of ZBB as
we see them. However, we have one last item for discussion: the costs of the ZBB effort, and the related
question, do the benefits outweigh the costs?

The problem in addressing the second part of the question is that ZBB is its own worst enemy. As we know, its major claim is that it undertakes zero-base reviews of programs. But actually, experience to date with ZBB reflects very little data on which to judge the merits of this claim. As we have noted, the Georgia experience certainly indicated no shift in the allocation of resources as a <u>direct</u> result of using ZBB. In addition, data from other states are spotty as to results in this area: for example, in a survey conducted in 1976 by the National Association of State Budget Officers, only two out of eleven states with some form of ZBB in existence reported any change in allocation as a result of ZBB. In Idaho, 10% of zero-base reviews "resulted in a substantial and significantly different approach to the operation of the program and reduced the required budget."[49] And,

> In Rhode Island, the ZBB approach has been ...at least partially responsible for (a) the elimination of 1300 positions from the state roster; (b) maintaining the reduced employment level during the past 18 months; and (c) allowing for the reallocation of funds from institutional to community programs (the shifting of priorities within the existing resources).[50]

In any case, if one measure of success is applied to the ZBB effort, i.e., the number of "obsolete" or "inefficient" programs wiped away, then certainly ZBB doesn't seem to pay for itself. Immediately, then, a conclusion seems to be warranted -- not unlike the one made of the USDA experiment with "zero-base budgeting" -- that the costs of the effort are high and the returns minimal at best. We believe this is to be unfair criticism and an unwarranted conclusion of the ZBB experience, <u>at least at this stage in its development</u>. The returns from "wiping away" programs in the public sector as a result of the ZBB effort will be slim, mainly because, as we alluded to previously, the triad of interests for continuance of a program (agencies, Congressional support, and clientele groups) are powerful and seriously handicap ZBB. (The prospects for zero-base reviews of new or prospective prospective programs are much brighter of course.) For its own sake, then, we would hope that ZBB does not trade on the number of programs it manages to abolish. It will certainly lose that contest. If ZBB can play down this part of its effort, its true benefits -- the ones we have cited -- will be made clear. Thus, we believe any "costs" of ZBB should more properly be netted against these benefits and not the unlikely benefit accruing to the number of standing programs it abolishes.

And what are the costs of ZBB? Excluding the USDA experiment -- and that experiment bears little connection with the recent, Pyhrr-like ZBB efforts -- no real analysis has been made of the direct costs of implementing ZBB. However, they are no doubt substantial, particularly in the first year: preliminary data reveal the costs could increase as much as 100 percent over the prior year's, non-ZBB-oriented budget preparation.[51] Like many other, similar, labor-intensive operations though, there is apparently a "learning curve" (learn by doing) associated with ZBB, i.e., time spent in budget preparation under a ZBB process drops after personnel become acquainted with it. This was observed and documented in the Georgia experiment.[52]

In addition to any direct costs involved in the ZBB effort, the question of opportunity costs should also be assessed. For when program managers and higher management now become intimately involved in the budgetary process, they all could be doing something else. They are foregoing opportunities by doing ZBB. Since the ZBB process is specifically designed to draw these persons into the budgetary process in a much more substantive way than before, we must conclude that the costs in this area will also be substantial. Once again, though, we might expect a learning curve to develop. Whatever the case, we are on less stable ground in assessing these costs than in determining direct costs: no data of any kind in the experience of ZBB to date exists for this area. It should be noted, moreover, that such costs may vary considerably from agency to agency depending on the vigor each agency's managers and management bring to the ZBB effort.

The third area of costs in the ZBB effort is, for want of a better term, the psychological costs associated with implementing another "budgetary method" within the bureaucracy. Agencies may balk mightily at what they feel is another "gimmick" foisted upon them in the name of "resource allocation efficiency." Here again, the nature of the costs have never been assessed, but they may well be staggering. When the initial bloom is off ZBB, and after it is realized that in some (maybe many) cases the allocation of resources is no different than before, ZBB may lose much credibility

-114-

within government. Agencies may view it as just another
waste of time. The "costs" associated with this revul-
sion may well be intolerable, and as the ZBB process
grinds on relentlessly, it may well engender a good
deal of desertion from the more established principles
of public management. How does one measure those
costs?

It should be obvious that any analysis of the cost
of ZBB is extremely tenuous now. No one simply knows
how much time and effort implementing ZBB will cost --
including the "surplus storage problems"! -- or the
more intangible opportunity and psychological costs.
What would appear judicious is that the process pick
and choose its way through its first year (or perhaps
two years). Heavy emphasis should be placed on the
feedback process, and perhaps experimental designs for
ZBB efforts be undertaken with selected agencies. The
District of Columbia government has chosen to pursue
this direction for example. What might be appropriate
in this connection in the Federal establishment would
be the implementation of a full-scale ZBB effort in the
Executive agencies along the schedules designed by
Congress for implementing "sunset" reviews of these
agencies in that body. (We shall comment on this
further in the next chapter.) Cost data from such
experimental efforts could be useful in determining
the range of costs that would occur in a government-
wide ZBB effort.

Further, in assessing the costs of the ZBB effort,
serious consideration should be given to obvious areas
where cost reductions could occur. One area of high
cost is associated with the preparation of decision
packages. Reducing the number of packages prepared --
particularly where it might not have any deleterious
effect on the process -- might be called for. Since we
view the zero-base reviews of programs as the least
beneficial area of ZBB, one possibility might be the
elimination of the Minimum Level decision package,
after, say, the initial year and the program has survived its zero-base review. After the first year,
zero-base reviews might occur then only periodically,
such as when there occurs a change in top management
within an agency. Of course such reviews would always
occur on proposals for new programs. Elimination of
the Minimum Level decision package in the sets of
decision packages might reduce costs in the preparation
of the decision packages and perhaps without any
apparent serious effects. In this connection, for

example, the analysis done of the Georgia ZBB effort
noted that "not a single instance was found" in the
Georgia FY 1973, 74, and 75 budgets "where a function
received less funds than it had in the previous fiscal
year budget."[53] Thus, the Minimum Level package
could really have been eliminated. In the New Mexico
ZBB effort this actually occurred: after several years
of the ZBB process, one major modification that was
made was the "abandonment of the level of effort below
the present base."[54] Some may argue that this is not
then "zero-base budgeting." This is not necessarily
true. Elimination of the Minimum Level decision
package would occur only where the benefits accruing
to its preparation were minimal; that is, in those
cases where the package was not prepared on a new program, or where top management had already previously
reviewed the justification for the program.

In any case, much more needs to be learned of the
cost side of the ZBB effort. And when confronting this
question we will still be left with the related one --
how much is "good" budgeting worth? It may well be that
ZBB may just be one alternative -- and perhaps a more
costly one -- in the road to "better" budgeting. Serious study, together with an adequate feedback system of
ZBB costs in selected agencies, needs to be undertaken
before the process is fully functioning and developed
government-wide. Only then can we begin to address
whether ZBB might be "worth it."

FOOTNOTES

CHAPTER FIVE

[1]Peter Pyhrr, Zero-Base Budgeting; A Practical
Management Tool, (New York: John Wiley & Sons, 1973),
p. 99.

[2]Harry S. Havens, "MBO and Program Evaluation,
Or Whatever Happened to PPBS?", Public Administration
Review, XXXVI (January/February, 1976), 40.

[3]Allen Schick, "A Death in the Bureaucracy: The
Demise of Federal PPB," Public Administration Review,
XXXIII (March/April, 1973), 147.

[4]The Department of Health, Education, and Welfare
was one agency in particular that viewed MBO in these
terms.   The Operational Planning System was DHEW's
version of MBO.   "With OPS added to the operating
cycle," the DHEW Handbook on OPS proclaims, "when each
agency lays out its requests for resources, it also
defines clear, measurable objectives indicating what
it intends to accomplish with those resources during
the fiscal year. As a result, internal HEW decisions
(and OMB and Congressional decisions as well) on resource allocations can be made on the basis of results
expected from a given amount of resources." See U.S.
Department of Health, Education, and Welfare, "Operational Planning System Handbook" (Washington: DHEW,
March, 1972, processed).

[5]Chester A. Newland, "Policy/Program Objectives
and Federal Management: The Search for Government
Effectiveness," Public Administration Review, XXXVI
(January/February, 1976), 20.

[6]Frank P. Sherwood and William J. Page, "MBO and
Public Management," Public Administration Review, XXXVI
(January/February, 1976), 7.

[7]David Novick (editor), Current Practice in Program Budgeting (New York: Crane, Russak, 1973), p. vii.

[8]U.S. Congress, House of Representatives, Committee
on the Budget. Hearings Before the Task Force on Budget
Process, 94th Cong., 2d sess. (Washington: Government
Printing Office, 1976), p. 53.

[9]George S. Minmier, An Evaluation of the Zero-Base
Budgeting System in Governmental Institutions, Research

Monograph No. 68 (Atlanta: Georgia State University, School of Business Administration, 1976), p. 154.

[10]Ibid., p. 155.

[11]Ibid.

[12]Ibid., p. 131.

[13]Ibid., p. 135.

[14]Peter Pyhrr, "The Zero-Base Approach to Government Budgeting," Public Administration Review, XXXVII (January/February, 1977), 8.

[15]John Saloma, The Responsible Use of Power (Washington: American Enterprise Institute, 1964), p. 32.

[16]Minmier, Zero-Base Budgeting, p. 180.

[17]Ibid., p. 181.

[18]John Lafaver, "Zero-Base Budgeting in New Mexico," State Government, XLVII (Spring, 1974), 108-112.

[19]Committee on the Budget. Hearings Before the Task on Budget Process, p. 78.

[20]Havens, "MBO and Program Evaluation," p. 43.

[21]Jong S. Jun, "A Symposium on Management by Objectives in the Public Sector: Introduction," Public Administration Review, XXXVI (January/February, 1976), 3.

[22]Peter F. Drucker, "What Results Should You Expect? A Users Guide to MBO," Public Administration Review, (January/February, 1976), 18.

[23]Pyhrr, Zero-Base Budgeting; A Practical Management Tool, p. 180.

[24]Minmier, Zero-Base Budgeting, p. 167.

[25]Lafaver, "Zero-Base Budgeting in New Mexico," p. 112.

[26]David W. Singleton, et al., "Zero-based Budgeting in Wilmington, Delaware," Governmental Finance, V (August, 1976), 28.

[27]Drucker, "What Results Should You Expect?", p. 18.

[28]Charles L. Schultze, The Politics and Economics of Public Spending (Washington: The Brookings Institution, 1968), pp. 94-95.

[29]Pyhrr, Zero-Base Budgeting; A Practical Management Tool, p. 189.

[30]Ibid., p. 119.

[31]Ibid.

[32]Ibid., p. 34.

[33]Schick, "A Death in the Bureaucracy," p. 147.

[34]Ibid., p. 148.

[35]Sherwood and Page, "MBO and Public Management," pp. 10-11.

[36]Ibid., p. 7. For an interesting discussion of the psychological effects on subordinates under a hierarchically controlled MBO process see Harry Levinson, "Management by Whose Objectives?", Harvard Business Review, XLVIII (July/August, 1970), 125-134.

[37]Ibid.

[38]See for example comments in James McGinnis, "Pluses and Minuses of Zero-Base Budgeting," Administrative Management, XXXVII (September, 1976); and Thomas Murray, "The Tough Job of Zero Budgeting," Dun's Review, CIV (October, 1974).

[39]See particularly his analysis of the "implementation problems" at the "Governor's Review and Budget Bureau Management" level. Pyhrr, Zero-Base Budgeting; A Practical Management Tool, p. 133.

[40]Minmier, Zero-Base Budgeting, p. 182.

[41]Ibid., pp. 183-184.

[42]Pyhrr, Zero-Base Budgeting; A Practical Management Tool, p. 158.

[43]Ibid., p. 2.

[44]Allen Schick, "The Road to PPB; The Stages of Budget Reform," Public Administration Review, XXVI (December, 1966), 243-258.

[45]Pyhrr, Zero-Base Budgeting; A Practical Management Tool, p. 153.

[46]See Michael J. Scheiring, "Zero-base Budgeting in New Jersey," State Government, XLIX (Summer, 1976), 178, and Lafaver, "Zero-Base Budgeting in New Mexico," p. 112.

[47]Lafaver, "Zero-Base Budgeting in New Mexico," p. 109.

[48] In this connection, for example, one concern of the Congress in its confirmation of Bert Lance as head of OMB was his receptivity to the idea of releasing to Congress agency budget requests previously submitted to the OMB. Also, legislation has been introduced into the 93rd, 94th and 95th Congresses to provide statutory authority for Congressional requests for such submissions. Another, more recent indication of this interest occurred during the budget cycle in Congress for the FY 1978 budget, particularly during the appropriations phase. Specifically, in the report accompanying the HUD-Independent Agencies Appropriations Bill, the Appropriations Committee commented on the FY 1978 budgets of the National Aeronautics and Space Administration and the Consumer Product Safety Commission, which had been submitted to Congress under a ZBB format. (NASA's ZBB effort was directed only at the Research and Program Management portion of its budget.) The Committee noted that these were just test cases -- initiated at the direction of the Committee -- and that these agencies' FY 1979 budget justifications (like those of all other agencies) would be submitted to Congress "in the regular format." However, the Committee "want[ed] to make it clear that if any of the ZBB submissions are requested of the agencies [i.e., the agencies' FY 1979 budgets prepared for the OMB], including priority ranking of decision packages, full cooperation will be expected from the agencies and the OMB." See U.S. Congress, House. Committee on Appropriations. Report (#95-380) to accompany H.R. 7554 (Washington: USGPO, 1977), p. 18.

[49]Allen Schick and Robert Keith, "Zero-Base Budgeting in the States," Library of Congress, Congressional Research Service, August 31, 1976 (processed), p. 15.

[50]Ibid., p. 16.

[51]Minmier noted that 78% of departmental budget analysts felt that the "time and effort" in budget preparation "increased considerably" under the first year of ZBB implementation, and all analysts felt that the "time and effort" had increased at least some. See his Zero-Base Budgeting, p. 159. The analysis of the Wilmington, Delaware, ZBB effort cites a net increase of "100 percent in the cost of preparing the budget." Singleton, "Zero-Base Budgeting in Wilmington, Delaware," p. 29.

[52]After three years of ZBB, however, almost one half (44%) of the analysts still felt that "much greater" time and effort was required under ZBB in comparison to the previous incremental budgeting system. Only 4% felt there was "slightly less" time and effort expended than before.

[53]Ibid., p. 173.

[54]Lafaver, "Zero-Base Budgeting in New Mexico," p. 110. A major factor in this abandonment was however that the state began to run surpluses in its budgets. One basis for implementing ZBB -- scarcity in resources -- became absent.

CHAPTER SIX

PROBLEMS AND PROSPECTS

Earlier, we noted how process alone does not make for more rational budgeting. Zero-Base Budgeting, as process, must confront this reality and attempt to have purpose triumph over technique. In this connection, we present here certain comments -- some in the form of half-conclusions or half-recommendations based on what the experience has been to date, and some in the form merely of observations, since very little evidence can be drawn upon -- that might be helpful as ZBB evolves over the next several years.

Information Saturation

First, and perhaps of major importance, is the fact that ZBB, like budget innovations before it, must confront the problem of the massive amount of paperwork that will be created as a result of the process. This will be the specter that always haunts ZBB and the one single factor -- if there can be one -- that will vitiate benefits of the system. For ZBB trades on its ability to develop and present data; at the same time the system could easily get lost in the welter of such data.

The problem has two dimensions: information saturation outside the agencies (at the Federal level, the OMB and Congress) as well as saturation within the agencies themselves.

First, there can be little doubt that ZBB as process can be done in agencies.[1] The problem comes however in getting the results of ZBB out of the agencies,
that is, getting the data that are generated and the
ZBB priority rankings into a meaningful system for decision-makers at the Executive Office level. Thus, one
aspect of the problem is the ability of ZBB analysis
within an agency to make that quantum leap into the
central budget office of the state or the Federal government, complicated of course by the fact that other
agencies' ZBB analyses will be trying to do the same
thing at the same time. For if the information saturation problem is to be avoided at the Executive Office
level, some mechanism must be provided for the results
of agencies' ZBB analyses to be incorporated into the
central budget office's budget presentation. This problem -- in its simplest form, precluding the chief executive from getting involved in "decision packages"
and "priority rankings" and yet at the same time deriving
the maximum amount of benefit from the conduct of zero-
base reviews within agencies -- is crucial to the system's viability. Further, it has already become the
basis for much of the criticism of why ZBB cannot be
done, at least at state and especially Federal levels.
For example, Wildavsky, in his analysis of the ZBB
effort in Georgia, commented that the mechanism for budgetary decisions by the governor under a ZBB process
was actually not very different from that under pre-
ZBB.[2] The governor still relied on "summaries" provided him by the Office of Budget and Planning and made
incremental decisions on the budget. Implicit in such
criticism is that as we move from one level of government to another (local to state to Federal), the information saturation problem becomes more critical and the
extent to which a chief executive can claim to have made
a "zero-base review" of all programs is problematical.

While we would agree with Schick and Keith that such
criticism misses the point since the appraisal of ZBB
focuses only on improvements in the budgetary process
at the chief executive's level,[3] there is still no deny-
ing that ZBB does have a problem in making the agencies'
zero-base analyses meaningful at higher levels of
decision-making. In smaller units, such as local governments, the problem is not that crucial. In these cases,
mayors and/or city managers can become intimately involved in the process of ZBB, and actually city councils
can rerank decision packages. Certain aspects of these
procedures have occurred in Garland, Texas and Wilmington, Delaware where ZBB provided the basis for the budgets

of these cities.[4] However, in larger governmental units
(state and Federal government), the link that exists
between decision packages/priority rankings within
agencies and the central budget office as well as the
chief executive of that government is unclear. Pyhrr
provides no help in this area either. Even his recent
comments on the role of ZBB in government ignores or
assumes away this crucial link.[5] In Georgia, "Summary
Analyses" have been relied upon to provide the results
of the ZBB process within agencies to the Executive
level. In Texas, "Agency Summaries" are utilized. However, the extent of what these"summaries" include or
how they are used has not yet been probed, nor has their
specific role in the ZBB process clearly been brought
out. Accordingly, what the prospects are in this area
cannot fully be determined at this time.

As ZBB evolves (particularly at the Federal level),
what appears likely is that it will be the OMB that
will come more and more to specify from agencies just
what information it requires from ZBB reviews in these
agencies. And this will come only as the system grows.
One particular direction which we feel has merit would
be the specification by the OMB of the display by
agencies of major tradeoffs among programs under different budget scenarios. This would leave the mechanical
processes of ZBB within agencies, not to mention much
of the information saturation. (Needless to say, there
would of course be nothing to preclude the OMB from
examining any or all of an agency's decision packages
and priority rankings to determine the reason for the
tradeoffs.) These tradeoffs, or, to return to a more
appropriate term, the display of "opportunity costs"
in various levels of an agency's budget, would constitute in large measure the basis for the OMB's budget
presentation to the President. Therefore, it may well
be the display of the opportunities foregone under
different agency budget scenarios that would provide
the link between the ZBB process in agencies and decision making at a higher level. Once again, then, we
view the display of opportunity costs -- this time at
a much higher aggregated level -- as primary in the ZBB
process, and a possible way to avoid information saturation at the chief executive level.

There is a second dimension to the information
saturation problem: this time as it relates to the
ZBB process within agencies. We have already alluded
in the last chapter to one area where saturation might
be controlled: reducing the number of decision packages

prepared. Thus, after the initial year's zero-base review of a program, and after the program has survived
Congressional review, serious consideration might be
given to cutting down on the incremental levels of decision packages, or, at the very least, gauging the incremental levels around which decision packages are
prepared to more realistic alternatives (say, 100%,
105% and 110% of last year's base, rather than 70%,
100%, and 120%). Under such circumstances, the packages would take on more meaning and avoid program managers' exasperation at having to submit what would in
substance be -- we would bet -- virtually the same
"Minimum Level" decision package each year.

Another way in which exasperation attendant to information saturation might be muted within agencies is
by being selective within agencies -- once again, only
after the initial year's zero-base review was conducted
-- in requiring what programs/functions/services are to
develop "alternative ways" of performing the same activity in decision packages. "Alternative ways" for many
programs/function/services in the public sector is a
different problem than "alternative ways" in the private sector. In the former, there are most frequently
no alternatives, simply because the goods/services are
public or quasi-public goods/services which the government provides because of market failure to provide for
them. There are few alternative "ways" for, say,
addressing the funding of basic research in this country, or the provision for the acquisition of new weapons systems used in our national defense, or for the
court system. Therefore, in such areas it serves no
useful purpose to continue to include such information
in decision packages. Inclusion of such information
on a continuous basis may be useful, however, in the
service and support related activities of many programs, such as in-house computer and health services,
security and maintenance, printing, etc. In these
cases, "alternative ways" of performing the same func-
tion/service might be displayed yearly since there are
realistic alternative ways of performing them.[6]

There are certainly other areas that can be explored to prevent information from swallowing up the
ZBB participants within an agency. We have touched on
just two of the more obvious. For example, while some
states use various types of back-up "displays," "schedules,"and "forms" which accompany decision packages,[7]
extensive use of such accompanying data may well "turn-
off" the ZBB participants at the much larger Federal

level. Thus, ZBB at this level may well turn out to be a very simple system.

Another area which might be explored after the first year is to revise the concept of what constitutes a "decision unit" for which decision packages would be prepared. The result would be that the organizational level at which decision packages are prepared and first ranked would be raised, with the obvious benefit of decreasing the total number of packages prepared. While this might seem to be heretical to the ZBB gospel, it appears to pose no real threat to the ZBB process. This actually occurred in the Georgia effort, with no apparent breakdown in the results emanating from the review of programs.[8] We should add, however, that if such a course is taken, the packages that are prepared should address realistic increments. It serves little purpose to have such packages prepared around, say, levels such as 110%, 120%, and 130% of last year's appropriation, since when ranking occurs top level management may be confronted with "all or nothing" situations. The increments should be finer-grained to allow decision makers to choose among realistic levels for such large programs.

In any case, our discussion merely points out several directions that might be pursued. What we have attempted to bring out is the fact that if ZBB is to trade on its ability to display much-needed information for decision makers, then both the manner in which the information is presented as well as the amount must be made meaningful. Only then will the resultant increase in information, that will inevitably accompany the ZBB process, be tolerated by all participants in the interest of the higher order of benefits which they perceive.

Inadequacy of Information

There is another side to the information problem that should be seen: there may actually be a lack of the right kind of information generated in preparation for the development of decision packages. As is obvious, ZBB requires that a significant amount of information be available to the program directors who prepare decision packages. Therefore information systems must exist within an agency to support ZBB. Benefits, costs, impacts and recommendations for program changes must be based on actual data and not merely hazy judgements if

they are to result in improved performance. This
again points in the direction of quantification. Hard
data which can be quantified provides a better basis
for judgement than do nebulous narrative explanations.
The observation is often heard as to how hard it is to
measure certain benefits or outcomes of programs. Indeed there are cases where this is true. Nevertheless,
it is often difficult to quantify because either objectives have never been established or measures of output
and effectiveness have never been devised. The idea
that a program cannot be quantified should be accepted
only when it can be clearly proven that a program manager knows his program objective and knows what he is
seeking to accomplish. Failure to develop quantified
data is often a failure to utilize internal management
information as much as it is the inability to obtain
data.

Management and Managers' Support of ZBB

A key factor in ZBB is involvement at all levels
of the organization in the process. There is a tendency
for headquarters or top level personnel to assume that
they can develop decision packages for all activities
in the organization. Such a course is to be avoided.
How far down in any organization ZBB decision packages
should be prepared is of course negotiable but as a
rule of thumb it should extend to the lowest level
program manager. This is preferable even if functional
managers or program directors must consolidate decision
packages into a second level decision package. As an
example, if an agency has seven scientists in different
parts of the country doing research on cancer, it would
be sound practice to have each of these seven individual
researchers submit a decision package type of input to
the program manager so that he could develop his own
total decision packages for cancer research. Similarly
in military structures, it would be preferable if each
installation or post submitted decision packages on its
activities which could be consolidated at an intermediate or command level in turn for submission to a
headquarters level. ZBB will function in a meaningful
sense only if (1) it becomes a routine way to do things
(2) it has the support of all levels of the organizations (3) it benefits all the participants. Unless all
participants to the process perceive some benefit from
the system it is not likely to result in basic, meaningful information being developed and integrated into
decision packages. In the last analysis poorly prepared

decision packages can negate all the well conceived
plans of top management.

ZBB and the Needs of Agencies

Anyone who has ever read of the struggle in the
late 1960's between the State Department and the Bureau
of the Budget to implant PPBS within that department
will realize the problem of trying to graft government-
wide a highly structured ZBB.[9] ZBB must be geared to
the individual agency method of making decisions. As a
result no one single method of ZBB can be applied across
the entire government.

We have presented one basic model for use but certain of these elements are subject to variation. As an
example, we offered a system of ranking in priority
order and the selection of which decision packages were
reviewed by higher authorities was decided on a percentage basis. The percentage could vary between differing
elements of the organization but nevertheless a percentage factor was the determining criterion. Another
possible alternative for consideration could be based
on dollar amounts. As an example, if an agency has
four reviewing levels above the program manager, the
first review level would study all decision packages
and only send those that involve the expenditure of
more than $100,000 to the next higher level. The second
level would limit its reviews to all packages in the
agency involving $100,000 or more. In turn the first
review level would have final decision authority to
approve expenditures of $100,000 or less. The second
review level could similarly develop a cut-off point of
$250,000. Below that level, review level two would have
final authority but above that level it would be required to submit the packages to level three. In this
manner each higher level concerns itself only with larger
and larger commitments of resources. The top review
level then would be concerned only with major expenditures of as an example $1,000,000.

Such an alternative model enables the workload
resulting from ZBB to be distributed in accordance with
an organizational hierarchy and saves the time of the
top level of the organization for only major expenditures. Another alternative would deal with the degree
of discretion involved in performing a program. If a
program is mandated by law, approval authority within
a given percentage of deviation could be delegated to a

first or second level review. Such a procedure would
work as follows. If a legally required program was
projected not to deviate $\pm$ 10% from last year's level
it could be routinely approved. Larger deviations would
require higher level decisions even if legally mandated.
Such a review by the highest approval level would take
the form of deciding whether or not legislative changes
should be requested. A similar approach could be taken
for decision packages on fixed costs e.g., utilities,
maintenance of real property. There is little question
that these costs must be met but significant deviations
in fixed costs offer consideration as to whether or not
alternative methods for meeting fixed costs should not
be considered e.g., a switch from oil to natural gas
for heating, or performing maintenance by in-house labor
or contract labor.

The basic idea remains that the system must meet
the needs of management and not vice versa. If the
system in and of itself becomes merely a driving force
for make-work it is better left unimplemented. Care
must be taken however to determine which level of management benefits from such an exercise. A lower level
of an agency may oppose ZBB analysis for fear that it
will expose certain pet projects to scrutiny. Top management must retain the options to insure that lack of
benefit is really pervasive at all levels of the organization before it condemns ZBB.

ZBB and Reorganization

As we have repeatedly noted, ZBB emphasizes the
management function of budgeting: the analysis of inputs and outputs under a predetermined objective. It is
certainly an exhaustive system in this regard, but its
chief limitation is that by <u>itself</u> it does not address
either effectiveness questions confronting government
(that is, impacts), or broader policy options that occur
in an environment of changing needs. Performance
measures are its strength in trade, and, as the analysis
on the New Mexico ZBB effort brought out, "without a
great deal of care, performance measures often show how
busy people are rather than the cost-benefit of their
activity."[10]

Thus from both an <u>intra</u> as well as <u>interagency</u>
standpoint, ZBB breaks down. In the former, the basis
for an agency's budget -- the decision packages --
are prepared by disparate "gut levels" within an agency.

-130-

And such levels are by their very nature myopic for the most part: they have a tendency to see only their own programs and not much further. In one sense then, an agency's top management, by ranking packages which have been prepared for it, is a captive of decisions already made.[11]

The ZBB process also provides no mechanism for examining interagency efforts or broader policy issues and programmatic thrusts that cross from one agency to another. The decision packages within agencies are entire unto themselves: packages in each agency address a particular aspect of a problem -- but nothing more.[12] Thus, for example, at the Federal level various agencies, bureaus and offices undertake programs in behalf of American Indian economic development. However, how does one compare the marginal value of packages say, in the Department of Interior's Bureau of Indian Affairs, with the ones in the Office of Minority Business Enterprise and Economic Development Administration of the Department of Commerce, with those in the Small Business Administration, with those in the Office of Native American Programs of the Department of Health, Education, and Welfare, and with those of the Indian Program offices of the Departments of Agriculture and Housing and Urban Development? The same may be said of the diverse programs the Federal government funds in many other areas -- research and development, community development, and health to name only three. Under the ZBB process, the decision packages in each of the agencies are ranked with other packages within the agencies. Any marginal analysis among packages that does occur occurs only at that level. But where is the mechanism for addressing the programmatic issues or policy options that span agencies? Priority rankings within agencies -- at least small agencies -- may uncover duplication and redundancies among programs, but there is serious doubt whether the process can by itself uncover substantial duplications/redundancies in large agencies, or particularly among agencies.

This parochialism on the part of agencies, which results in having the agencies see most problems as a reflection of their own self-interest, was particularly noted in the Texas ZBB effort. As one analysis notes:
This fragmentation creates three classes of extra-agency problems: increasing duplication of services, gaps in needed services, and inefficient divisions of labor. These problems impede achievement of overall state policies

and objectives. ZBB did not create these
problems, but the method of defining decision packages does little to improve the
situation.13

In fairness to the ZBB advocates, however, we
should add that they do not run from the problem. Pyhrr,
for example, in his book devotes an entire chapter to
his suggested remedy: ZBB should be "reinforced" by a
PPB System. And, indeed, in five of the eleven states
where ZBB is currently used, it is used in conjunction
with a program budgeting system already in place.14 In
Montana, for example, under its "Priority Budgeting
System," ZBB is the last of three distinct "but closely
related" phases. The first two, "policy formulation"
and "long range planning," provide the basis for "trans-
lating the Governor's policy initiatives and multiyear
plans into the executive budget."15

There is another method, however: reorganization
of government agencies with similar functions. Indeed,
owing to the fact that the disastrous experiences of
PPB are still fresh even six years after its official
demise in the Federal establishment, this may be the
only viable alternative at that level of government.
Further, the interconnection between ZZB and reorganization is a close one. In Georgia, for example, while
much is made of ZBB, "it was the Executive Reorganization Act of 1972 [which reduced drastically the number
of agencies] that has been credited with reallocating
the state's financial resources during this period."16
However, at the same time, then-Governor Carter noted
that "the detection of need for consolidating similar
functions within state government is made from zero-
base budgeting technique."17 A similar connection can
be observed in other governments which have attempted
ZBB. In Garland, Texas, for example, "just prior to the
introduction of ZBB, twenty-eight municipal departments
were organized into five administrations."18 And the
problem cited earlier in connection with the state of
Texas ZBB effort may be as a result of the failure of
the executive and legislative branches to opt for organizational changes in conjunction with ZBB.19

This is not the place to discuss the direction that
government reorganization should take. Such a reorganization of similar functions has been proposed before --
most recently in 1971 under President Nixon in his plan
for super-departments -- and it is one way proponents
of a non-PPBS approach to government feel that analysis

of programmatic overlaps among agencies can be accomplished.[20] All that can be said is that since ZBB has quite obviously a problem in addressing higher or overlapping needs within some agencies and among all agencies, one remedy may be reorganization. Thus, what the the prospects are for ZBB in this regard are still vague. However, the swiftness with which President Carter has moved to initiate government reorganization at the Federal level, together with his equally swift charge to Executive agencies to undertake ZBB, certainly seems to indicate that both efforts will proceed apace with each other.

ZBB and the Legislature

In the previous chapter we commented that while ZBB may be an executive budget process, if the legislature and the chief executive are to play out their symbiotic roles in setting priorities, then the legislature should give more than tacit recognition of ZBB. In those states where ZBB has not produced the full measure of success that was expected, a major reason has apparently been the failure of the legislature to accept budgets prepared under the ZBB process.

Equally important is the fact that an executive budget process must let the legislature in, and allow sufficient time for the executive to groom legislative acceptance of the process. The days of PPBS, where for the most part Congress ignored the process, should not be repeated. Charles Zwick, then Director of the Bureau of the Budget, laid out a major cause for this lack of acceptance: "Those of us who were involved in the early days of the PPB System were so preoccupied with internal executive branch problems and interfaces that from time to time we forgot there was a legislative branch of government."[21]

However, the early signs for ZBB in this regard at the Federal level augur well. In recent years, Congress has taken special interest in executive budget formulation. Legislation introduced over the last three Congresses to require agencies to submit to Congress their "OMB Budgets" reflects the dimension of the interest. ZBB should benefit from this interest. Also, as we have noted, Congress itself has introduced its own form of ZBB, so-called "sunset" legislation. The basic feature of the most recent and prominent bill, S. 2 (originally entitled the "Sunset Act of 1977" but later

renamed the "Program Evaluation Act of 1977"), is that
while the term "zero-base review" is not used (unlike
the bill introduced in the 94th Congress, S. 2925),[22]
the legislation would call for actions by Congress that
are tantamount to such a review. Accordingly, unlike
the problems affecting previous budget innovations,
ZBB's backing **by** Congress is one of the most encouraging
prospects in its future.

We might only add in this connection, however, that
in the interest of preventing information saturation in
Congress, and also in achieving maximum benefit from
"zero-base reviews" in both branches, one prospect may
be to tie Congressional sunset reviews more closely
with executive ZBB along the lines of the schedules for
such reviews detailed in the legislation. For example,
under S.2, by September 30, 1979, and progressing through
the next five years, certain government programs would
be reviewed. In the first round, that is, those to be
subject to a "sunset" review by September 30, 1979, the
programs are National Defense, Recreational Resources,
Farm Income Stabilization, Disaster Relief and Insurance,
Health Research and Education, and Veterans Housing.
By September 30, 1980, another set of programs would be
reviewed. Perhaps more extensive reviews of programs --
we are reluctant to use the word "true" zero-base reviews
-- could be performed by the Executive on each program
in the year prior to its coming up for Congressional
sunset review. In the case of our example, in 1978 a
more extensive review of National Defense, Recreational
Resources, Farm Income Stabilization, etc. would be
performed by the Executive during the ZBB cycle in
that year. If the program survives both the Executive
ZBB review and the Congressional sunset review, then
the program might not be subject to an Executive zero-
base review for another five years. Such a program
would still be in the annual Executive ZBB process
of course, but the analysis for those next four years
would concentrate on the incremental aspects of the
program's budget rather than on zero-base aspects.
Further, as a new series of programs comes up for a
sunset review each September 30th, and as the ZBB process in the Executive departments evolves, more adequate feedback can be achieved for the benefit of
Congress as to what exactly it may desire from the
Executive to assist it in its own review of programs
during the next round. Once again, this would enhance
the roles of both the executive and legislature in
their desires to coordinate the budgetary process.

[1]What constitutes a ZBB "review" may differ among
agencies. Also, the specification of when a ZBB process
is in place may be open to some interpretation. For
our purpose here, we are most comfortable with the
definition of the process by the National Association
of State Budget Officers: "Zero base budgeting is a
system by which ... programs and activities are organized and budgeted in a detailed plan which focuses
review, evaluation and analysis on all proposed expenditures rather than on increases above current expenditure levels. The purpose is to determine whether
each activity warrants continuation at its current level
or a different level, or should be terminated. This
focus requires a priority ranking of all programs and
activities in successively increasing levels of performance and funding, starting from zero." Allen Schick
and Robert Keith, "Zero Base Budgeting in the States,"
Library of Congress, Congressional Research Service,
August 31, 1976 (processed), Appendix, no page.

[2]Aaron Wildavsky, Budgeting: A Comparative Theory
of Budgetary Processes, (Boston: Little, Brown & Co.,
1975), pp. 295-96.

[3]Schick and Keith, "Zero Base Budgeting in the
States," f.n. 5, p. 23.

[4]See David L. Leininger and Ronald C. Wong, "Zero-
base Budgeting in Garland, Texas," Management Information Service, Report No. 4A, (April ,1976) and David
Singleton, et al, "Zero-based Budgeting in Wilmington,
Delaware." Governmental Finance, V, (August, 1976).

[5]See his, "The Zero-Base Approach to Governmental
Budgeting," Public Administration Review, XXVII
(January/February, 1977), 1-8.

[6]Actually, it was in this area that ZBB was inaugurated -- and perhaps works best. In his seminal work,
the article in the Harvard Business Review that brought
him to the attention of those in the field of government
administration, Pyhrr notes that "The first thing
to understand about zero-base budgeting is that it is
best applied to service and support areas of company
activity, rather than manufacturing operations proper."
"Zero-base Budgeting," Harvard Business Review, XLVIII

(November/December, 1970), 112.

[7]In the FY 1978 Budget Procedures and Instructions for Georgia, for example, there was required thirteen supplemental "schedules" and forms providing backup to decision packages and rankings within a department. These provided information on such things as motor vehicle equipment purchases, per diem and fees, computer charges, and personal services. See State of Georgia, Office of Planning and Budgeting, "General Budget Preparation Procedures FY 1978 Budget Development "(Atlanta: 1976).

[8]George Minmier, An Evaluation of the Zero-Base Budgeting System in Governmental Institutions, Research Monograph No. 68 (Atlanta: Georgia State University, 1976), pp. 76-84.

[9]See for example Frederick C. Mosher and John E. Harr, Programming Systems and Foreign Affairs Leadership (New York: Oxford University Press, 1970).

[10]John Lafaver, "Zero Base Budgeting in New Mexico," State Government, XLVII (Spring, 1974), 112.

[11]This is not always the case however. For example, during FY 74 and FY 75, when there was first an increase and then a decrease in the availability of funds for the state, Governor Carter directed that new decision packages be prepared to cope with the marginal adjustments he had to make. Thus, he just didn't shift the cut-off lines to include or exclude the marginal packages. Minmier, Zero-Base Budgeting, p. 169.

[12]It has been suggested that computer systems can aid in maintaining records of each decision package, and thus allowing for a broader perspective of similarly-related packages among agencies. While we do not question the role of computer technology in assisting in the ZBB process -- it would be particularly useful in constructing "what if" situations under alternate budget scenarios for an agency -- we seriously question (at least at the Federal level) the benefits accruing from the creation of a centralized, monumental data bank of government decision packages.

[13]"The Budget -- A State's Real Operating Plan," An Evaluation Conducted by Research and Planning Consultants, Austin, Texas (undated).

[14]Schick and Keith, "Zero-Base Budgeting in the States," p. 25.

[15]See U.S. Congress, Senate, Committee on Government Operations, _Compendium of Materials on Zero Base Budgeting in the States_, 95th Cong., 1st sess. (Washington: Government Printing Office, January, 1977), pp. 356-64.

[16]Minmier, _Zero Base Budgeting_, p. 156.

[17]Interview with Jimmy Carter, _Ibid_.

[18]Leininger and Wong, "Zero-Base Budgeting in Garland, Texas," p. 1.

[19]See for example in this connection comments by Michael H. Granoff and Dale A. Kinzel, "Zero-Based Budgeting: Modest Proposal for Reform," _Federal Accountant_, XXIII (December, 1974), 56.

[20]See for example, Leonard Merewitz and Stephen H. Sosnick, _The Budget's New Clothes_ (Chicago: Markham Publishing Co., 1971), p. 274.

[21]U.S. Congress, Joint Economic Committee, _Economic Analysis and the Efficiency of Government._ _Hearings_, Part I, 91st Cong., 2nd sess. (Washington: Government Printing Office, 1970), p. 165.

[22]S. 2925 was reported but no action was taken by the Senate during the 94th Congress.

CHAPTER SEVEN

Zero-Base Budgeting in the Federal Government*

The election of President Carter brought zero-base budgeting to the Federal government in 1977 just as it did to the State of Georgia the year after his election as Governor in 1970. Despite the obvious fact that the budget of the Federal government is significantly larger than the Georgia state budget, President Carter stuck to his campaign promise and mandated on February 14, 1977 that all agencies participate in the process. The U.S. Office of Management and Budget (OMB) issued instructions on April 19, 1977 implementing the President's desire, which provided the agencies of the Federal government with a basic framework for Zero-Base Budgeting (ZBB) not unlike the Pyhrr-developed system that had been utilized in Georgia.[1] Through the summer of 1977, numerous budget and program analysts throughout the Federal government labored to master the new system within their respective agencies. The product of their effort was their agencies' Fiscal Year (FY) 1979 budget submissions to the OMB in September, 1977.

While most Federal agencies and offices met their assigned deadlines, the budgets that were submitted to OMB varied in quality and content just as they did in the pre-ZBB days.[2] Agencies encountered more than the usual number of problems in budget preparation, most of which stemmed from unfamiliarity with ZBB techniques and uncertainty about OMB directives. Since ZBB will continue to be utilized at Federal, state and local levels for the foreseeable future, it is perhaps a good time to

---

*This chapter first appeared as an article published in the Government Accountants Journal (Spring, 1978). The authors thank the editors of the Journal for permitting it to be used in basically the same form in this book.

look back -- and identify some lessons learned from the first year's experience with ZBB.[3] We have broken down our observations into three broad areas, with comments made on particular aspects of the ZBB process in these areas.

Structure of the Process

o Identifying Decision Units

For the most part, it appears that agencies were able to maintain the fundamental characteristics of a ZBB system: that is, identification of <u>decision units</u> around which significant budgetary decisions are made, the preparation of <u>decision packages</u> which reflect alternative levels of funding for the units, and <u>ranking</u> of such packages to display agency priorities.

However, a major problem arose as to the level at which individual decision units were first identified within an organization. Agencies had a not-unreasonable fear of "information saturation" created as a result of ZBB. To thwart this saturation, however, they may also have thwarted one of the major purposes of ZBB -- to bring program managers, the "untapped reservoir" as Pyhrr calls them, into budget preparation. Stated simply, to avoid being inundated by packages pyramiding to them from each of the programs in the "guts" of an organization, in several agencies top and higher level management established the decision units relatively high in the organizational structure. And when this occurred, program managers, who are closest to their programs, were not allowed adequate input into the construction of decision packages. Now this is not to say of course that consolidated decision packages should not be prepared at higher aggregated levels in an organization. But the agencies' setting of the <u>initial</u> decision units at these higher levels was tantamount to preparing consolidated decision packages first.

Many decision units should be identified and many decision packages prepared initially rather than merely a few at high levels of aggregation. Top management should require detailed decision units and decision packages prepared for every area in which program managers are required to make significant budgetary choices. By such a process, management can have detailed data available to back up consolidated decision packages during its own internal decision-making process. If the opposite course is taken (prepare few consolidated packages and respond with detail data only if asked), the short turn around time available for such responses will generally result in headquarter's or budget office personnel preparing detailed packages from broad gauge packages. It is preferrable to utilize the program managers to prepare decision packages that are consolidated into fewer packages as the packages ascend the organizational ladder, so as to utilize the detailed knowledge that can only be provided from the working level.

But stating that decision packages should be prepared at low levels does not mean that decision units can be identified indiscriminately. One obvious constraint is that meaningful data must be available from which to prepare decision packages. In identifying decision units consideration must be given to the availability of accounting data or other such meaningful financial data which agencies report. An accounting or management structure which captures data is a necessary prerequisite of a ZBB effort.

Preparation and Review of ZBB Materials

o Beginning ZBB Early

The Calendar Year (CY) 1977 preparation of the Fiscal Year 1979 budget started much too late to enable agency analysts to perform serious assessments of the ZBB data. The late start in CY 1977 was primarily due to the late issuance of OMB Bulletin 77-9, which instructed agencies in the ZBB process. For its part, OMB had a justifiable reason for its lateness, since it had to revise the existing "A-11" and this simply took time. So much for the late 1977 start. What should an agency do in "starting early" with its ZBB process?

Top management in each agency should use the first quarter of each calendar year to develop its goals, objectives and broad priorities. Such an early start has much to recommend it. For example, goals and objectives -- which afterall address questions of impact and effectiveness -- should be more the province of the planning and policy analysis stages of the budget cycle. And these stages precede the budget preparation stage. The goals and objectives of programs should already be in place by the time the actual preparation of decision unit "overviews" and decision packages occurs. Unless agency program managers and budget officers are aware of top management's preferences and areas of emphasis, they cannot adequately address the preparation of decision packages and the ranking that follows. By this early consideration of goals and objectives a budget strategy can begin to take shape early in the calendar year. And the ZBB preparation, which will occur during the summer, will key to this strategy.

Ideally, a well developed Planning-Programming-Budgeting (PPB) System in an agency will provide the vehicle for transmitting such preferences to the staff. In the absence of a functioning PPB System, or some similar alternative system, a general guidance letter from the head of the agency to the assistant directors, budget officers and program managers would be a step in the right direction in getting these participants to think about the upcoming ZBB information requirements early. Thus, while ZBB is undeniably a "bottom up" approach to budgeting, it is at the same time essential that ZBB be initiated with "top down" guidance.

In a similar connection, it appears that addressing alternative ways of performing a program -- a vital element in ZBB -- should also be considered early in the year. As with goals and objectives, consideration of this area should also occur at the pre-preparation stages of the budget. Our research also indicates that few if any alternative ways to programs can be realistically addressed at the individual decision unit levels. Or if they are addressed, much duplication occurs. Under such circumstances, it is simply not cost-effective at these levels. Rather, consideration of alternative ways may be more properly assessed at higher levels of consolidation in an organization, where it can be placed in its proper context -- namely, the exposition of the rationale for program balance and strategy for this higher consolidation level. As we said, this strategy should occur before the actual preparation of the ZBB budget.

o Drafting Realistic Alternative Levels of Funding

The original conception of ZBB focused around decision packages built on three alternative levels of funding: a Minimum level, a Current level, and an Improvement level. Supposedly, the Minimum level, which in theory at least is to be set by each program manager, is the level below which the program cannot drop and yet still remain viable. However, most agencies find it difficult to have the Minimum level packages seemingly "well-up" from the program managers' level. As a result, some arbitrary percentage was usually assigned to all Minimum levels of an agency. For example, in the FY 1978 budget request to Congress, the Environmental Protection Agency's Minimum level was arbitrarily set at 25% below the actual budget request to Congress;

the U.S. Public Health Service's Minimum level (for the FY 1979 budget submission to the OMB) was set at 80% of the FY 1978 appropriation for the agency.[4] Also, some agencies felt that for many programs the Minimum and Current levels should be the same. For example, in the Consumer Product Safety Commission's FY 1978 budget justification to the Congress, about one third of the programs had the Minimum and Current levels identical.[5]

Needless to say, most agencies did not wish to present a realistic Minimum level for fear of actually later being given such a level of funding.[6] However, Minimum levels <u>are</u> needed, and once again agencies seem to have lost sight of one of the most important aspects of ZBB. <u>For it is at the Minimum level where the actual zero-base review of the program occurs; it does not occur at any of the additional incremental levels.</u> If no Minimum level is shown, or not addressed realistically, then a zero-base review of the program cannot be claimed to have occurred.

Yet exhortations to "go Minimum" may be of little use; a "second-best" solution to this critical ZBB problem may be more realistic. One method of making the Minimum level more realistic is to have the head of an agency assign to each next level of subordination (say, the Assistant Director level), a Minimum dollar amount for each of these levels. This amount might be some percentage -- say, 80% -- of the directorate's current appropriation. At the same time, however, Assistant Directors are allowed to construct Minimum level packages around <u>any</u> funding level for the individual programs (decision units) in that directorate. The only constraint is that these Minimum level packages cannot exceed the Minimum level assigned to the directorate as a whole. In this way flexibility is achieved within each of the directorates: each Assistant Director can shift resources within the directorate to ascertain some approximate Minimum level for each individual decision unit, and at the same time the Director of an agency is able to counter arguments that he/she is arbitrarily setting the Minimum level for each program. Perhaps this method is a sub-optimal one, but it certainly deserves consideration as one way of addressing a difficult aspect of ZBB.

Another alternative method may be to have the agency head arbitrarily set a Minimum level for each program, but at a level that is so far below the Current level as to cause little fear in the program manager that he/she would be given such an amount.

Thus the director of an agency may set the Minimum level at, say, 40% or 50% of Current. Under such circumstances, program managers may reason that "they probably couldn't give me as little as that," thus allaying the primal fear of all managers that their program will be cut.

In any case, the point should be reemphasized that zero-base reviews of programs have to occur, and that the Minimum level exercise has to be taken seriously. ZBB is not ZBB without this emphasis.

As with preparation of the Minimum level package, there are also problems attendant to the preparation of incremental packages. And these problems stem from the inability (or unwillingness) on the part of most participants in the ZBB process to be realistic. Top level management and budget directors should work with program managers to identify alternative levels of effort that reflect reasonable and realistic expectations of funding. The greater the number of program managers there are throughout an agency preparing similar decision packages, the greater is the need to insure that each manager is using the same criteria for preparing improvement as well as decremented levels of funding in decision packages. As an example, if a government service is provided at the Current level on the basis of 40 hours per week of service, programmatic guidance should be issued for program managers to develop alternatives around 30, 35, 45 and 48 hours per week. In some cases, programmatic guidance of this sort may be preferable to stating alternatives in terms of percentages of funding. Similarly, alternatives for vehicle maintenance cycles, temperature settings in buildings, number of grants authorized, tons of material shipped, process time for claims, number of meals served, and many other such items can be developed to assist the program managers in preparing decision packages that reflect agency alternatives. The basic idea in all of this specialized guidance is that program managers should be called upon to cost alternative levels of service/performance that are consistent with top management's goals and objectives, rather than merely permit their imagination to select what they see from their perspective as program managers.

In this connection, one recommendation is that there should be an insistence by top management that so-called "Intermediate" (decremented) level decision packages be prepared.[7] (The Intermediate level is the level between Minimum and Current.) This should be accomplished even in spite of the fact that like

-144-

the preparation of the Minimum level package (and for the same reason), program managers balk at addressing decrements below Current. However, this reluctance also reflects a moving away by program managers from another key element of ZBB: ZBB is as much "incremental budgeting" as anything, and "incrementalism" means not only increments above Current but decrements below as well. Constructing Intermediate levels offers the decision-makers an opportunity to identify realistic trade-offs among programs while rejecting program termination. Given the nature of political support for most government programs, the most that can be actually accomplished is not program termination but reducing the level somewhere below what is being considered at present.

This problem of addressing realistic increments is applicable to Improvement level packages as well. One basic problem uncovered in some agencies -- too late in the ZBB exercise it should be added -- was that Improvement level packages were prepared at too high a percentage of Current (say, 115% and 125%). The agency head found that when he/she began to rank such unrealistic Improvement level packages, the more realistic funding ceiling for the agency (the OMB "mark") came up very quickly. (The same may be said about constructing consolidated decision packages at unrealistic levels and ranking them.) The result is that under an agency-wide ranking done in line with the ceiling for that agency, some programs would get an Improvement level of funding and some would not. Because this situation is likely to be intolerable to any agency head (since there may be many individual projects within these programs that deserve Improvement levels of funding), an agency head has a tendency at the final stages of the ZBB process to want to "split" decision packages. Or if splitting does not occur, some juggling of fiqures is attempted in these prepared packages. But such an exercise vitiates the ZBB process, since this splitting or juggling at the last minute cannot but be detrimental to the goals and objectives of the decision unit as an entity.

The implications of this experience with Improvement level packages are clear and the remedy is obvious. If decision units (or consolidated decision units) are set at a rather high organizational level in an agency, and if the decision packages (or consolidated decision packages) built around these units form the basis for preparation of the agency ranking sheet, then the Improvement level packages should be set -- if need be arbitrarily by higher management under a percentage scheme -- around the margins of what the agency might reasonably and realistically expect to get for that funding year. Thus, under tight budget constraints, Improvement level packages would be written around increments of, say, 102% (of Current), 104%, 106%, 108% and 110%. Improvement level packages beyond these levels would represent "wish lists" of an agency's budget (i.e., 115%, 125%).

    o Treatment of Cost-Growth Items in ZBB

        Another area where considerable concern has been expressed is that of how to handle cost-growth items such as pay raises and inflation. One recommended way is that decision packages should be prepared on a constant dollar basis using the current year as the base (FY 77 for the FY 79 budget). The central budget office rather than the individuals preparing the decision packages should add pay raises and inflation to both the other years displayed (FY 78 and FY 79 in the FY 79 budget). This precludes individual program managers having to project their own estimates of pay increases and inflation into individual decision packages. In addition to consistency it also permits analysis of comparable data. It is difficult for decision-makers within an agency and in OMB to analyze year-to-year program changes if they must constantly factor out pay raises. In addition, it provides a sound strategy for program managers to limit the changes between years and between different levels in decision packages in the budget year to actual programmatic changes, rather than require them to justify increases over which they have no control.

        The degree to which pay increases present a problem to agencies in their ZBB preparation is, of course, a function of how large personnel costs are in relation to their total budget. To many departments it represents a major portion of the budget. A sample display of how this could be accomplished is as follows for a single package at, say, the Current level:

	1977	1978	1979
Administration	$1.55M	$1.57M	$1.58M
FY 1978 Pay Raise		.25M	.27M
FY 1979 Pay Raise			.30M
	$1.55M	$1.82M	$2.15M

In the above case the program manager prepares his/her decision packages and defends the programmatic portion only, i.e., $1.55M, $1.57M and $1.58M. To disregard pay raises completely will result in a budget that does not represent an agency's total funding request and is out of line with the agency's budget submission to Congress. If ZBB is to be effective, it must meet this latter requirement, namely, it must be readily convertible into the agency's non-ZBB budget submission to Congress. Therefore, any pay raises and, if permitted, inflation must be included.

o Need for "Feedback" in the Final Stages of ZBB

Another area in ZBB which seems to have lagged is the one of "feedback." It can only be reemphasized that ZBB is built on program managers' input; without this input and support the entire system is a house of cards. And "feedback" is especially crucial at the final stages of the ZBB process in an agency. Program managers who prepare decision packages should be made aware of what top management decided regarding their packages. Unless there is "feedback," program managers are likely to feel that preparing decision packages is a meaningless exercise. Since ZBB attempts to utilize "participatory management" techniques, the flow of information must be two-way or else an adverse reaction is likely. Management must recognize that ZBB, like all other attempts to involve workers in decision-making, must be careful to avoid the impression that it is merely an attempt to make workers feel well. Results must be perceived as flowing from the participation. Because ZBB involves program managers in the budgetary process more than ever before, it must be handled with caution.

A good "feedback" mechanism will provide the preparer of the decision packages with not only the results but the rationale for top management's decisions. This indeed will result in a major amount of work. Nevertheless it is a necessity.

Ranking Process

o Need to Rank All Packages

Another question that has arisen is whether or not the ranking process should extend from a zero-base or whether the "highest priority," say the Minimum level packages of an agency's budget request, should be exempt from prioritization. Not a few agencies balked at attempting to rank Minimum level packages against one another. This was clearly observed also in the FY 1978 experimental agency ZBB efforts done at the request of the Congress. For example, in its FY 1978 budget submission to Congress, the Environmental Protection Agency's Office of Energy, Minerals and Technology "made the assumption that each of the 39 subtasks should receive a 'lowest budget' before any subtasks should receive a first increment."8 However, the incongruity of such a situation was not lost on the Senate Committee on Appropriations. In reviewing EPA's budget request the Committee noted that while the Administration had placed a strong emphasis on using coal as a substitute fuel, EPA's priority rankings of all Minimum level packages before any Improvement level packages actually negated this thrust. While the Committee acknowledged that the ZBB exercise for EPA was an experimental one, still it felt that such a lack of realistic effort toward prioritization was detrimental to the ZBB process. The Committee was not sparing in its comments:

> Unless each agency and department is willing to make decisions that require the deletion of some activities entirely in order to fully fund more rewarding tasks, the zero-base budgeting approach will not be a priority setting mechanism in the fullest sense. While it is always easier to keep all subtasks going at minimal levels of funding, it is also an extremely inefficient way to marshal the resources of the Federal Government.9

The House Committee on Appropriations noted a similar problem with the Consumer Product Safety Commission's experimental ZBB budget in FY 1978. CPSC claimed that it could not rank the packages "because of the interdependence of agency programs and the lack of a management information system."10 However, after hearing testimony the Committee believed that a ranking of CPSC packages "was not only possible but desirable." In fact, as the Committee points out, "it was the six budget activities translated into operating programs that the Committee ranked in making its 1978 budget recommendation from the Commission."11

The theory behind any agency's reluctance to rank Minimum level packages is why bother increasing workload by placing a priority on what is obviously going to be funded. But to re-emphasize what the House Committee has stated -- all decision packages should be ranked. The obvious reason for this is that if a portion of the budget is exempt from prioritization, there will be a tendency for some program managers to hide low priority or hard-to-defend packages in this area. Permitting this to happen within an agency often merely delays the day of reckoning. For once the budget submission is reviewed by OMB, and if these "soft" or undefendable programs are surfaced, then an agency will often be hard pressed to justify them.

Another reason for listing all packages in priority order is for top management to view the totality of its resource commitments in a systematic manner. If ZBB has a major advantage it is that it systematizes what has often been a unsystemmatic

process, i.e., justifying the base of any given year's expenditures. If nothing else top management should want to see how
program managers and mid-management rate the importance of all
ongoing activities within their areas of responsibility. Of
course the major controversy and effort will focus on packages
at the margin where there is a question as to whether or not
they will be funded. Nevertheless ranking all packages is the
preferable approach.

o ZBB, OMB, and an Agency's "Mark"

As we noted earlier, a recurring problem in ranking was
the fact that Improvement level packages were not addressed at
realistic levels. As a result, a "shoehorning" attempt often
occurred at the time of the final agency-wide ranking; that is,
a splitting of decision packages or juggling of figures so as
to allow some additional (Improvement) level of funding for
virtually all programs. (It appears that ZBB ranking created
one of the few Pareto-optimum situations ever actually observed,
one where all programs win and none lose!) As we said, one way
to avoid this "shoehorning" is to identify decision units at
lower organizational levels in an agency and/or prepare more
realistic Improvement levels of funding around these units.

However, ZBB would also be well served by OMB's not giving
agencies a fixed "mark" to shoot at for the agencies budget
submissions to OMB. By not displaying this ceiling to agencies,
OMB would force the agencies to devote true time and effort to
ranking, and not just concentrating -- almost exclusively it
seemed -- at trying to pull a mix of packages into the OMB
ceiling that will satisfy the most number of people in an agency.
Without an inflexible "mark," agencies will be less likely at the
last minute to split packages or juggle funds within them so as
to accommodate within the "mark" bits and pieces of programs
found in each of these packages.

o Building an Agency-Wide Ranking from Scratch?

Another area that seemed to cause some concern was the
construction of a final agency-wide ranking. It would not be
unreasonable to assume that most heads of agencies did not look
forward to such a task. However, there is no reason for top
management to start from scratch in the ranking. One aid is to
have each of the next subordinate organizational levels (say,
Assistant Directors) rank all the agency packages first and an
average ranking for each decision package be displayed. This
ranking sheet is then used as a basis for the agency head in
his/her ranking.   The procedure has much going for it since it
allows the agency head to see priorities within an agency from
different viewpoints.

CONCLUSION

The overall impression of the first year of ZBB is that despite unfamiliarity with the system, late issuance of instructions and guidance by the OMB, and a certain amount of inherent resistance to change on the part of the bureaucracy, the process functioned mechanically. The substance of the question however is not whether new formats were completed and suspense dates met as required, but whether or not ZBB penetrated the decision-making procedures of Federal agencies. Did, in reality, agencies examine their programs from a zero-base and were budgetary decisions any different because of ZBB? On this point we are not particularly optimistic.

Perhaps it is too much to expect that agencies would alter the way they construct budgets in the short space of one year. After all, budgetary strategies, tactics, and relationships develop over many years. In addition most agencies probably view their existing approach to budgeting as satisfactory if not outright successful. Therefore agencies are likely to question why tinker with success. Having said this however, we must conclude that there is one aspect of ZBB that appears to have made some progress in penetrating the budget preparation process. Decision-makers in agencies appear to have relatively quickly adapted to considering alternative levels of funding for programs. This is a significant departure from the concept of one fixed budget number as the only acceptable level of funding. How useful alternative levels are of course depend on the realism of the alternatives offered. Nevertheless, once decision-makers integrate this approach and method of thinking into their standard bag of decision-making devices we will have come a long way procedurally, at least as far as we were intellectually in 1952 when Verne Lewis wrote his famous article on alternative budgets.[12]

Next year's effort at ZBB should provide certain experiential benefits and learning improvements merely because the technique will not be a totally new one as it was in 1977. This should simplify the effort to some degree. Overall, the key to the success of ZBB will still rest with the top management of all Federal agencies. They simply must find ZBB useful and so inform their staffs. Lacking this top level emphasis ZBB is likely to remain a mechanical process no matter how much President Carter extolls its virtues. The Congress can of course be helpful in this area. If Congressional committees examine budgets from the standpoint of alternatives it would behoove agency heads to be prepared to discuss and defend their budgets from that viewpoint. At this time it is still too early to judge if this will be the case. To venture a guess we expect that Congress will do just that. The knowledge that agencies have this great number of decision packages listing alternative levels of funding in a priority ranking is probably too great a temptation for Congress to resist and too great a risk for agencies to attempt to hide or deny.

As one noted author on budgeting has observed, "...the Federal budget process is but another manifestation of the nature of humans to create institutions to administer public resources in the face of two conflicting objectives of use and control."[13] ZBB at this stage fits into this mold and is the latest such attempt to reconcile the two objectives of use and control. The jury is still out on how effective it will be in performing this role but one thing appears certain -- we will have at least three more attempts to try it.

CHAPTER SEVEN

[1]Peter A. Pyhrr, <u>Zero-Base Budgeting; A Practical Management Tool for Evaluating Expenses</u> (New York: John Wiley & Sons, 1973).

[2]On October 11, 1977, the OMB asked each Federal agency and department for an assessment of the ZBB exercise just completed (i.e., for the FY 1979 budget submission to OMB). This was directed in <u>OMB Bulletin 78-1</u> and responses were due into OMB by November 11.

[3]To obtain an idea as to the scope of the problems, types of difficulties and methods used to overcome them, the authors interviewed approximately 125 budget officers and program managers from various Federal agencies. These interviews constitute the bulk of the research data which form the basis for this article. (The interviews were conducted in conjunction with the authors' ZBB seminars given during 1977 under the auspices of the George Washington University, Washington, D.C.) Also, the authors examined the record of hearings of Congress and considered appropriate committee reports, which reflected the experimental agency ZBB submissions to Congress for FY 1978. Finally, the authors examined, where available for public consumption, internal agency guidance for ZBB preparation. However, it must be emphasized that the views here are the authors' own and no attribution is implied to any agency, especially the National Science Foundation and the Department of the Army.

[4]See U.S. Congress. Senate. Committee on Appropriations. <u>Report to Accompany H.R. 7554</u> (Senate Report No. 95-820), 95th Cong., 1st sess.; and U.S. Department of Health, Education, and Welfare, Public Health Service, Office of Administrative Management, <u>Zero Base Budgeting for the Public Health Service</u> (April, 1977; processed).

[5]U.S. Congress. House. Committee on Appropriations. <u>Report to Accompany H.R. 7554</u> (House Report No. 95-380), 95th Cong., 1st sess.

[6]However this may be an agency bug-bear, at least if experience is any indication. For as the analysis of the Georgia ZBB experience shows, during the first three years of ZBB in that state "not a single instance was found where a function received less funds that it had in the previous fiscal year budget." See George S. Minmier, <u>An Evaluation of the Zero-Base Budgeting System in Governmental Institutions</u>. Research

Monograph No. 68. (Atlanta: Georgia State University, School of Business Administration, 1976), p.173.

[7]OMB *Bulletin 77-9*, The keystone of the Federal effort, states only that "when appropriate" a decision package set should include an Intermediate level.

[8]U.S. Congress. Senate. *Report to Accompany H.R. 7554* p.10.

[9]Ibid.

[10]U.S. Congress. House. *Report to Accompany H.R. 7554*, p.14

[11]*Ibid.*, p.16

[12]Verne Lewis, "Toward a Theory of Budgeting," *Public Administration Review*, XII (Winter, 1952), 42-54.

[13]Thomas C. Stanton, "Conceptual Underpinnings of the Federal Budget Process," *Federal Accountant*, XXIV, No. 4 (December, 1975), 51.

CONCLUSION

There is a story told -- apocryphal, we believe, but we're not quite sure -- of a certain budget analyst in one government agency some years ago who struck upon a particular budget innovation: it was called "historical incrementalism."

It seems that the analyst was assisting in the preparation of the long range plan estimates for the agency and commented that since the previous year's appropriation was $1,066 million, why not make the figures for the next five years, $1,215; $1,429; $1,776; $1,865; and $1,918 millions. He (or she) was of course immediately rejected as being a crackpot. However, strangely enough, these figures actually became the budget authority for his agency in these out years. He was vindicated.

The analyst prospered in his profession, no doubt because of his powers of prescience and his unique ability to divine the interrelationship between historical events and an agency's budget requests to Congress. Eventually, he went on to become the chief budget officer for a rather large bureau of another department. When last heard from, his current long range plan estimates for his bureau were keyed to events in Chinese history. People around him refer to this as his "Oriental Period."

We mention this only to burst, in this final word, any balloons on Zero-Base Budgeting. Performance budgeting, PPB, MBO, ZBB, or what comes after, hold no special aura. What constitutes "better budgeting" is still largely indefinable. For after all, how does one measure the difference between the rightness of, say, $400 billion or $401 billion in new obligational authority requested? The question of the marginal value of an additional dollar spent on "battleships

155

versus poor relief" will always be with us.

It has been written that "ZBB is no panacea," or
that it "cannot be implemented by fiat." We would agree.
We might even add our own comment: "Zbb is no Rosetta
stone what somehow unlocks the secrets of good budgeting."
But so what?

All we can say is that ZBB is a product of the
times. As the 1920's -- and its cry for the return to
"Normalcy" -- demanded the Budget and Accounting Act
of 1921, as the 1930's and the descent of efficiency
experts on Washington demanded performance budgeting,
as PPB was tied to the hopes and programs of the Great
Society, and as MBO traded on the desires of the managers who inherited these programs, so "accountability,"
"responsiveness in government," and "openness in decision making," perhaps demand ZBB. Charles Beard's
comment in 1917 still holds: "Budget reform bears the
imprint of the age in which it originated."

In reality, ZBB adopts specific aspects of many of
its predecessors. One can see the similarities between
ZBB and performance budgeting, PPBS and especially
alternate budgets. ZBB also adopts elements of marginal
utility economics, welfare economics and cost benefit
analysis in its techniques. ZBB also attempts to avoid
some of the more obvious errors of its predecessors.
To be avoided are the reams of complex paper analysis
that helped to sink PPBS. Also to be guarded against
is decision-making that disregards political consideration and is based on such complicated mathematical
computations that only experts can understand them.

ZBB is increasing in significance because it is a
budgeting approach that promises to re-examine what
government does at the present time before embarking on
new ventures. It is not necessarily true that ZBB is con-
servative in outlook or designed to curb expenditures
but rather that it recognizes certain facts of current
political and economic life. These facts are that much
of the public feels that governments at all levels may
perhaps be trying to do too much and that economic
growth cannot be taken as an indisputable fact of life.
Like so many other important ideas it appears to be that
ZBB is an idea whose time has come. It remains to be
seen however whether the Federal government can adopt
ZBB on the scale needed to make it an effective instrument of budgetary politics. This will require a massive

effort to train budget-makers in the techniques of ZBB. Attempts to train personnel in techniques of PPBS were largely unsuccessful. ZBB on the other hand attempts to involve the most knowledgeable personnel to prepare analysis of those programs they know best. Only by building on an already existent base of knowledge can such a massive redirection of effort stand any chance of success.

ZBB will follow a yet undetermined path. However, if it does nothing other than once again make government look at itself a little more -- from the sacrosanct intelligence agencies to the equally sacrosanct social programs -- then it should be blessed. Who knows, it may even be fun. And for budgeting, that has to put you somewhere over the rainbow.

ZBB BIBLIOGRAPHY

BOOKS, MONOGRAPHS, AND PAMPHLETS

Cheek, Logan M. Zero-Base Budgeting Comes of Age. New York: American Management Association, 1977.

Georgia. Office of Planning and Budget. General Budget Preparation. Procedures, Fiscal Year 1978 Budget Development. Atlanta, 1976.

Hogan, Roy L. Zero-Base Budgeting: A Rationalistic Attempt to Improve the Texas Budget System. Austin: University of Texas, 1975.

Merewitz, Leonard and Sosnick, Stephen H. The Budget's New Clothes. Chicago: Markham Publishing Co., 1971. Chapter 5.

Minmier, George S. An Evaluation of the Zero-Base Budgeting System in Governmental Institutions. Research Monograph No. 68. Atlanta: Georgia State University, 1975.

Pyhrr, Peter A. Zero-Base Budgeting; A Practical Management Tool for Evaluating Expenses. New York: John Wiley & Sons, 1973.

Research and Planning Consultants (Austin, Texas). The Budget -- A State's Real Operating Plan. An evaluation. Austin, undated.

Schick, Allen and Keith, Robert. Zero-Base Budgeting in the States. Washington: Congressional Research Service, Library of Congress, August 31, 1976.

Schultze, Charles L. The Politics and Economics of Public Spending. Washington: The Brookings Institution, 1968. pp. 77-102.

Stonich, Paul J. Zero-Base Planning and Budgeting. Homewood, Illinois: Dow Jones-Irwin, 1977.

Wildavsky, Aaron. Budgeting: A Comparative Theory of the Budgetary Process. Boston: Little, Brown, 1975. pp. 278-296.

ARTICLES

Anderson, Donald N. "Zero-Base Budgeting: How to Get Rid of Corporate Crabgrass." Management Review, v. 65 (October 1976), pp.4-16.

Anthony, Robert N. "Zero-Base Budgeting is a Fraud," Wall Street Journal (April 27, 1977).

Axelrod, Donald, "Post-Burkhead: The State of the Art or Science of Budgeting." Review of Pyhrr's book, Public Administration Review, v. 33 (November/December 1973), pp.576-584.

Carter, James E. "Zero-Base Budgeting." Nation's Business (January 1977), pp. 94-96.

"Carter's Zero-Based Budgeting Netted No Real Saving, Georgia Officials Say." Baltimore Sun (April 11, 1977) p. 1.

Dean, Burton V. "Conceptual Problems in Implementing Zero-Base Budgeting." Paper Presented at the Spring Symposium -- The American Association for Budget and Program Analysis, George Washington University (March 1977).

Garbut, Douglas and Minmier, George S. "Incremental, Planned-Programmed and Zero-Base Budgeting." Public Finance and Accountancy (November 1974), pp. 350-357.

Granof, Michael H. and Kinzel, Dale A. "Zero-Base Budgeting: Modest Proposal for Reform." Federal Accountant, v. 23 (December 1974), pp.50-56.

Haider, Donald F. "Zero-Base; Federal Style." Public Administration Review, v. 37 (July/August 1977), pp. 400-407.

Hartman, Robert W. "Budget Prospects and Process." In
Setting National Priorities, The 1978 Budget, Joseph
Pechman (ed.). Washington: The Brookings Institution,
pp. 355-389.

_____. "Next Steps in Budget Reform: Zero-Base
Review and the Budgetary Process." Policy Analysis,
v. 3 (Summer 1977).

Havemann, Joel. "Congress Tries to Break Ground Zero
in Evaluating Federal Programs." National Journal,
v. 18 (May 22, 1976), pp. 706-713.

_____. and Cohen, Richard E. "Zero-Base
Budgeting and Sunset Legislation." National Journal,
v. 19 (April 2, 1977), pp. 514-520.

Hayward, John T. "Buzz Words Galore." Government
Executive, v. 8 (September 1976), p. 19.

LaFaver, John D. "Zero Base Budgeting in New Mexico."
State Government, v. 47 (Spring 1974), pp. 108-112.

Large, Arlen J. "Applying Zero-Base Budgeting." Wall
Street Journal (May 24, 1977).

Leininger, David L. and Wong, Ronald C. "Zero-Base
Budgeting in Garland, Texas." Management Information
Report, v. 8, no. 4A, International City Management
Association (April 1976).

Leone, Richard C. "How To Ride Herd on the Budget."
Nation, v. 222 (May 22, 1976), pp. 625-627.

Lewis, Hunter. Review of Pyhrr's book on ZBB.
Washington Post (January 9, 1977), p. K3.

Lewis, Verne. "Toward a Theory of Budgeting." Public
Administration Review, XII (Winter 1952), pp. 42-54.

McGinnis, James F. "Pluses and Minuses of Zero-Base
Budgeting." Administrative Management, v. 37
(September 1976), pp. 22-23.

Miller, Karl. "Zero-Budgeting Works in Yonkers, N.Y."
Government Executive (January 1977), pp. 39-40.

Minmier, George S. and Hermanson, Roger H. "A Look at
Zero-Base Budgeting -- the Georgia Experience."

Atlanta Economic Review, v. 26 (July/August 1976), pp. 5-12.

Murray, Thomas J. "The Tough Job of Zero Budgeting." Dun's Review, v. 104 (October 1974), pp. 70-72.

Muskie, Edmund S. "Effective Government: Our Next Big Challenge." National Journal, v. 8 (April 3, 1976), pp. 458-459.

Pyhrr, Peter A. "Zero-Base Budgeting." Harvard Business Review, v. 48 (November/December 1970), pp. 111-121.

_____. "Zero-Base Budgeting -- Where to Use It and How to Begin." S.A.M. Advanced Management Journal, v. 41 (Summer 1976), pp. 4-14.

_____. "The Zero-Base Approach to Government Budgeting." Public Administration Review, v. 37 (January/February 1977), pp. 1-8.

Scheiring, Michael J. "Zero-Base Budgeting in New Jersey." State Government, v. 49 (Summer 1976), pp. 174-179.

Singleton, David W. et al. "Zero-Based Budgeting in Wilmington, Delaware". Governmental Finance, v. 5 (August 1976), pp. 20-29.

Stanton, Thomas C. "Conceptual Underpinnings of the Federal Budget Process." Federal Accountant, XXIV, No. 4 (December 1975), pp. 44-51.

Stonich, Paul J. "Formal Planning Pitfalls and How to Avoid Them," parts I and II. Management Review, v. 64 (June 1975), pp. 4-11 and (July 1975), pp. 29-35.

_____. "Zero-Base Planning -- A Management Tool." Managerial Planning, v. 25 (July/August 1976), pp. 1-14.

_____. and Steeves, William H. "Zero-Base Planning and Budgeting for Utilities." Public Utilities Fortnightly, v. 98 (September 9, 1976), pp. 24-29.

"Ways to Make Uncle Sam Spend More Wisely." Nation's Business, v. 60 (August 1972), pp. 26-28.

"What It Means to Build a Budget from Zero." Business
Week (April 18, 1977), pp. 31-33.

Wildavsky, Aaron and Hammond, Arthur. "Comprehensive
versus Incremental Budgeting in the Department of
Agriculture." Administrative Science Quarterly, v.
10 (December 1965), pp. 321-346.

Wilson, Charles H. "Zero-Base Budgeting: Will It Work
and Is It Another Buzzword." Reprinted in Congressional Record (January 31, 1977), H627-633.

Wilson, James Q. "Zero-Base Budgeting Comes to
Washington." The Alternative: An American Spectator,
v. 10 (February 1977).

"Zero-Based Budgeting -- A Way to Cut Spending or a
Gimmick?" U.S. News & World Report (September 1976),
pp. 79-82.

"Zero-Based Budgets Offer Data, Spending Control."
Industry Week (January 12, 1976), pp. 48-50.

"Zero-Base Budgeting: One Way to Erase Needless Government Programs." Nation's Business (November 1976),
pp. 52-56.

U.S. GOVERNMENT DOCUMENTS

U.S. Congress. House. Committee on Appropriations.
Report to Accompany H.R. 7554. Washington: USGPO, 1977.

U.S. Congress. House. Committee on the Budget. Task
Force on Budget Process. Zero-Base Budget Legislation. Hearings. Washington: U.S. Government Printing Office (USGPO), 1976.

U.S. Congress. Senate. Committee on Appropriations.
Report to Accompany H.R. 7554. Washington: USGPO, 1977.

U.S. Congress. Senate. Committee on Government Operations. Government Economy and Spending Reform Act
of 1976. Hearings before the Subcommittee on Inter-
governmental Relations. Washington: USGPO, 1976.

U.S. Congress. Senate. Committee on Government Operations. Government Economy and Spending Reform Act
of 1976. Report to Accompany S. 2925. Washington:
USGPO, 1976.

U.S. Congress. Senate. Committee on Rules and Administration. Government Economy and Spending Reform Act of 1976. Report to Accompany S. 2925. Washington: USGPO, 1976.

U.S. Congress. Senate. Committee on Government Operations. Compendium of Materials on Zero-Base Budgeting in the States. Washington: USGPO, 1977.

U.S. Congress. Senate. Committee on Governmental Affairs. Program Evaluation Act of 1977. Report to Accompany S. 2. Washington: USGPO, 1977.

U.S. Department of Health, Education, and Welfare. Public Health Service, Office of Administrative Management. Zero-Base Budgeting for the Public Health Sector. Washington: U.S. DHEW, April 1977 (processed).

U.S. Office of Management and Budget. Bulletin No. 77-9, April 19, 1977, subject: Zero-Base Budgeting (processed).